Survival Training

for the Believer

Survival Training

for the Believer

Achieving and Maintaining
Spirit, Soul and Body Fitness

By Thomas Geier

Leeway Literary Works
Published by Leeway Artisans, Inc.

Book & Cover Design by Mykle Lee

ISBN: 978-0-9846698-9-9

First Edition
Printed in the United States of America.

Contents

INTRODUCTION   **1**

So What Should We Do?   3

LESSON ONE HUMAN TRICHOTOMY

Chapter One Separate Functions   **10**

Discipline Each Component   11

Spiritual Fitness   12

Readiness Required   13

Be On God's Side   14

Chapter Two Fitness of the Soul   **17**

Mental Health   17

Selective Study Essential   20

Mental Health Conclusion   21

Chapter Three Emotional Security and Stability   **22**

First Things First   23

Unsuitable Substitutes   24

Simplification Required   25

Chapter Four Reconciling Our Will with God's Will   **27**

Evidence Of Their Co-Existence   28

Discipline Has No Alternative   29

Physical Fitness   31

LESSON TWO IMPORTANCE OF PHYSICAL FITNESS

Chapter Five A False Concept   **36**

The Heart   37

Proper Weight   39

A Healthy Diet   41

Regular Exercise   43

Adequate Sleep   45
Abstain From Habit Forming Drugs   46

Chapter Six Managing Stress   **48**
Periodic Physical Examinations   50
Establishing Priorities   50

LESSON THREE THE FOUNDATION OF FAITH

Chapter Seven Faith Defined   **55**
From Where Does It Come?   56
Fear Not   58
Something to Trust In   60

Chapter Eight Discovering Truth   **64**
Perform the Condition   65
Biblical Promises   66
Trust and Obey   67

LESSON FOUR ADD GOODNESS TO FAITH

Chapter Nine Sow - Reap Principle   **73**
What You Are   75
What You Do   79
Three Essentials for Christian Leadership   83

Chapter Ten When Goodness is Lacking   **85**
Wisdom Required   86
What Throne?   87

LESSON FIVE ADD KNOWLEDGE TO GOODNESS

Chapter Eleven The Essence of Practical Knowledge   **95**
Does God's Way Really Work?   97
Further Evidence   98

Chapter Twelve What We Must Know To Be Saved   **100**
Knowing and Doing God's Will   102
Acquiring Knowledge   104

Chapter Thirteen Consequences of Ignorance or Disobedience of God's Word   **109**
The Safe Path in a Dangerous World   109
Hypothetical Situation   111
Conclusion   112

LESSON SIX ADD SELF-CONTROL TO KNOWLEDGE

Chapter Fourteen An Essential Element of Freedom   **118**
The Control Issue   119
Use The Forces at Work   122

Chapter Fifteen We Must Be Diligent   **125**
Refuse to Compromise   128
Guard The Back Door   128
Control Your Body   130

LESSON SEVEN ADD PERSEVERANCE TO SELF-CONTROL

Chapter Sixteen Wait Upon The Lord   **136**
It Requires Tenacity   137
It Takes Time   138
Becoming Beautiful   139

Chapter Seventeen Use Your Time wisely   **143**
Build Memorials   145
Practical Application   147
Fight The Good Fight; Finish The Race   148
Learn and Pursue Your Calling   150
Accept the Realities of Life   151

LESSON EIGHT ADD GODLINESS TO PERSEVERANCE

Chapter Eighteen What Godliness Is Not   **158**
The Freedom Issue   159
A Choice Is Required   160

Chapter Nineteen The Foundation Stones of Godliness   **163**
Discard Your Logic of What is Fair, Just, Reasonable & Effective   165
Lavish Love   165
Compassion For the Lost   166
Dealing With Rebellion   167
Accumulation of Wealth   168

Chapter Twenty It Gets Easier   **169**
Law of Reciprocity   170
Law of Use   170
Law of Perseverance   171
Law of Responsibility   172
Law of Greatness   173
The Law of Unity and Harmony   175
Law of Miracles   176

Chapter Twenty-One See Things Through God's Eyes   **179**
The Real Challenge   180

LESSON NINE ADD BROTHERLY KINDNESS TO GODLINESS

Chapter Twenty-Two Helping Those Incapable of Helping Themselves   **185**
Refusing to Help Those Who Won't Help Themselves   186
Providing Opportunities to Those Seeking a Chance to be Productive   187
Recognize and applaud achievement.   188

Chapter Twenty-Three Caring for Your Own Flesh and Blood   **189**
Use Positions of Authority for the Benefit of Others   191
Ask Questions, Then Listen Intently to the Answers   192
Raising God-Fearing Difference Makers   194

Chapter Twenty-Four Refuse to Gossip and Spread Unkind Rumors of Others   **196**
Forgiving Others of Mistakes, Insults and Offenses   197

Obeying Commandments Five Through Ten   198

Chapter Twenty-Five Just Being There   **199**

LESSON TEN ADD LOVE TO BROTHERLY KINDNESS

Chapter Twenty-Six Definition and Use   **203**
God's Version of Love   203

Chapter Twenty-Seven Rewards of Self-Sacrifice   **206**
Doing All He Could   207
Love of God and His Word   207
Putting Others Ahead of Self   209
Love Keeps Good Company   210
Summary   211

CONCLUSION   **213**

INTRODUCTION

Terrorism is the word, topic and paranoia of the day. Webster defines it as "the systematic use of terror especially as a means of coercion." We presently have our fill of contemporary examples such as the horrendous 9/11/01 attacks on New York City and Washington D.C., suicide bombings in Jerusalem, the West Bank and other sections of Israel, car bombings and rocket attacks in Baghdad and other cities in Iraq, train bombings in Madrid, assassination of political leaders, and on and on.

I challenge you to find a single daily newspaper that doesn't contain the word, or a world news program that at some point doesn't elaborate on some aspect of the topic or a recent relevant event. The media seems to believe that a profusion of discussion of the matter will produce the elusive solution, bringing about the eventual eradication of the violence. But I'm thinking that all of the commentary and rhetoric dwells solely on the symptoms rather than the root cause. And since those roots cannot be extracted, is there a solution?

I believe our contemporary "enlightenment" thinkers are ignorant of the root or origin of the problem, and few, if any, would even consider it if presented to them. Only those who believe in the literal interpretation of Scripture have the capacity to know and understand its ancient beginnings.

We find them in the fifteenth through eighteenth chapters of the book of Genesis when the Lord appeared to Abraham and promised him a son in his old age. But after a rather lengthy wait, his old and barren wife persuaded him to take matters into his own hands and make it happen. So he slept with Sarai's (name not yet changed to Sarah) Egyptian maidservant, Hagar, and had a son with her they named Ishmael. An angel of the Lord prophesied of this child that he would be a "wild donkey of a man; his hand will be against everyone and everyone's hand against him, and he will live in hostility toward all his brothers" (Genesis 16:12).

That was clearly not the son promised to Abraham by the Lord. His name was to be Isaac, and he would be born to Sarah when she was 90 and Abraham 100. He is the one who was to inherit all that God gave to Abraham, and to whose vast descendants would be the recipients of the everlasting covenant between the Lord and his father.

History affirms that the roots of today's Middle East turmoil and terrorism around the world were planted way back then. The Arab world has Ishmael as their father, while the Jews trace their ancestry back to Isaac. And the hostility and violence prophesied so many centuries ago continues to take center stage of much that consumes humanity today. It's tempting to wonder what life on this planet would be like at this moment if Abraham trusted fully in the Lord and refused to interfere in God's promise, plan and timing.

So if the prophetic utterances found in Scripture were literally fulfilled in that instance as well as in at least five hundred other occasions since then, should we not look there to see what lies ahead for us and our children? I concur with the beliefs and interpretations of Dr. Tim LaHaye, a noted author, minister and speaker on Bible prophecy. I love the way he and Jerry Jenkins fleshed out potential end time events in their fictional Left Behind series. And while I believe as they do that the New Testament Church (born-again believers) will be raptured prior to the Tribulation, it's obvious that progressively difficult times will be experienced until then.

David Wilkerson, the late Pastor of New York City's Times Square Church and founder of Teen Challenge, was--in my opinion--America's Jeremiah. In the letter accompanying his 3/29/04 teaching entitled A Christian In Name Only, he writes, "This message warns about difficult times ahead--things I have been warning about for a long time. But no trusting, praying Christian should be discouraged or upset by such prophetic warnings. God never has and never will forsake his children. We who love him need never fear. He has given us unbreakable promises of protection and provision."

So What Should We Do?

How does one prepare for such unpredictable calamity? Should we imitate many others and buy guns, gas masks and emergency bio-medical kits; and stock up on food, water and other supplies? Terrorism experts with comprehension of the real dangers we face imply, however, that these personal safety and preservation measures are akin to hunting bear with a stick.

So what can we do to protect ourselves, loved ones, neighbors and property? Is our invisible enemy invincible, or has he an achilles heel? How do we maintain our peace, poise, courage, contentment and composure when everyone around us is losing theirs?

There is no solution for those who refuse--or for some reason seem unable--to turn to God, submit to His will and ways, and learn and obey His Word. But all who walk daily with their Lord have a reliable and proven shelter to abide within.

The Bible says, "God is our refuge and strength, an ever present help in trouble. Therefore we will not fear, though the earth give way and the mountains fall into the heart of the sea, though its waters roar and foam and the mountains quake with this surging" (Psalm 46:1-3).

"He rescued me from my powerful enemy, from my foes, who were too strong for me. . . He brought me out into a spacious place; he rescued me because he delighted in me. . . For I have kept the ways of the Lord; I have not done evil by turning from my God" (Psalm 18:17, 19, 21).

That brings us to the purpose of this book. Matthew 24:10-13 tells of the increase of wickedness and the apostasy of the Church during the last days. The apostle Peter provides the best method for standing firm until the end. He says, "For this very reason, make every effort to add to your faith goodness; and to goodness, knowledge; and to knowledge, self-control ; and to self-control , perseverance; and to perseverance, godliness; and to godliness, brotherly kindness; and to brotherly kindness, love. For if you possess these qualities in increasing measure, they will keep you from being ineffective and unproductive in your knowledge of our Lord Jesus Christ" (2 Peter 1:5-8).

This is therefore a training manual for achieving and maintaining excellent spirit, soul and body fitness. Paul tells us in 1 Corinthians 9:24 that we need to run our race in such a way as to get the prize. And Peter defines that prize in the continuation of the above passage by saying, "Therefore, my brothers, be all the more eager to make your calling and election sure. For if you do these things, you will never fall, and you will receive a rich welcome into the eternal kingdom of our Lord and Savior Jesus Christ" (2 Peter 1:10,11).

Freedom from the anxiety presently gripping our nation and the rest of the world--such as that which caused a house fire awhile back when a woman microwaved her mail to destroy potential anthrax bacteria--is essential for the peace, serenity, energy and concentration required for achieving full readiness. "HE WHO dwells in the shelter of the Most High will rest in the shadow of the Almighty. . . You will not fear the terror of night, nor the arrow that flies by day, nor the pestilence that stalks in darkness, nor the plague that destroys at midday. . . . For he will command his angels concerning you to guard you in all your ways. . . 'Because he loves me,' says the Lord, 'I will rescue him; I will protect him, for he acknowledges my name. He will call upon me, and I will answer him; I will be with him in trouble; I will deliver him and honor him.'" (Psalm 91:1, 5, 6, 11, 14 & 15).

Moving back to Paul, he says, "Everyone who competes in the games goes into strict training. They do it to get a crown that will not last; but we do it to get a crown that will last forever" (1 Corinthians 9:25). SO LET THE TRAINING BEGIN!

LESSON ONE
HUMAN TRICHOTOMY

I AM NOT PRESBYTERIAN, but have informally participated in a few of their ongoing doctrinal debates. There isn't a biblical paradox nor topic inconsistently recorded in Scripture that has not been fervently debated by members of that denomination. While I disagree with some of their deductions, I applaud their diligent study of God's Word.

One of the least debated scriptural inconsistencies, in my mind, is one of the more important issues relative to practical application of Bible knowledge. A "trichotomist," such as myself, contends that we humans are comprised of three parts -- Spirit, Soul, and Body. 1 Thessalonians 5:23 states all three, and Acts 4:32 and Hebrews 4:12 distinguishes between soul and spirit. "Dichotomists," on the other hand, point to the numerous Old and New Testament passages that use one or the other in a synonymous manner. They conclude that we are therefore comprised of just two parts -- Spirit or Soul and Body.

I feel it's vital to differentiate between our spirit and soul. Evidence abounds that they are separate entities with distinct functions. Accordingly, consistent and progressive development of each requires varying methods and individual attention.

I once heard Evangelist Pat Robertson define our three separate parts on his 700 Club. He described our body as that which has material substance; is controlled by the physical senses; begins at conception, and ceases to exist in a functional manner upon our physical death. The spirit, on the other hand, is that which is invisible and capable of communing with God; existed prior to our physical reality, and lives on into eternity in heaven or hell. The soul, as distinguished from the spirit, is comprised of our mind, emotions and will; came into being at our physical birth, and simply ceases to exist upon death of the body;

and is that which enables the body and spirit to communicate and co-operate despite being diametrically opposed to one another.

A contemporary analogy readily understood by citizens of the computer age associates the body with the hardware components, the spirit with the data submitted, and the soul as the software. The computer machine and the information fed it have nothing in common. The operating program, however, enables them to relate to one another. When all three parts are produced, submitted and functioning efficiently, they are harmonious and beneficial to the user.

In a similar manner, our soul is interposed between the body and spirit, creating the paradoxical capacity of living concurrently in the physical and spiritual dimensions of life. The direction in which our total being advances is determined by choices made along the way. All such decisions are made within our mind, enforced by our emotions and transacted by our will. We must realize the importance of the soul's ability and purpose, and to understand how it's influenced in conflicting ways by our spirit and body.

Chapter One Separate Functions

The spirit exists deep within our being and is the only part capable of direct communication with God. It is here that His Holy Spirit abides within the individual who invites Him in and submits to His control. This submission is possible only when a consistent and substantial period of time is spent in Bible study and prayer. Our spirit is fed and strengthened by ongoing acquisition and application of scriptural knowledge, and fellowship with our Creator.

A well conditioned spirit exerts influence upon our thought process, which in turn charts the course our life will take. The physical body is influenced and led by its five senses, but can be brought under the control of a disciplined and determined will. An individual whose mind submits to a strong, healthy spirit is an "inside-out" person; one whose power source is deep within their being.

A weak and undernourished spirit, on the other hand, exerts little or no influence upon the mind, emotions and will. They in turn look out, rather than in, for guidance. It is at this point that deceiving spirits of Satan's legions acquire easy access through the sensual realm of the physical body. They then exert pressure on and dominion over the individual's mind. Thus an "outside-in" person is created; one who is directed and controlled by things of this world.

Those engaged in the spiritual and physical battle relative to being freed from destructive behavior understand this better than most. A particular man, ensnared for years by a pornography addiction, was asked by his mentor as to how he was doing. He responded by saying it felt like two large dogs were fighting within him. "Which one is winning?," inquired the counselor. "The one that I feed," answered the addicted man.

That insightful observation explains why it's urgent to comprehend our threefold composition, and realize these separate and distinct functions are intensely integrated with one another. Once we understand that, the need to persistently develop each in accordance with God's Word should be a no-brainer for all who are determined to do and be His will. The Lord stated it most clearly when He said, "My people are destroyed from lack of knowledge" (Hosea 4:6).

Discipline Each Component

Phillip Keller devotes a separate chapter to the need for nurturing body, soul and spirit in his A Shepherd Looks At The Good Shepherd And His Sheep. He says, "If in truth I am God's person; if Christ has in fact entered my life, my body belongs to Him: He resides there. My right to do with it as I choose has been abdicated. . . I no longer have any right to be overworked, overstressed, overfed, overindulged with drink, nor overcharged with sex. . .It is to be exposed fully and freely to the benefits of fresh air, sunshine, clean water, wholesome food, moderate exercise and adequate sleep. . .

"Turning to my soul with its mind, emotions and will, precisely the same principal applies. This is my person, now indwealt by the living Spirit of the living God. I shall not permit it to be cramped and contaminated by exposing it to such dusty trivia as newspaper propaganda, pornography, cheap debasing literature, hours of low caliber television programs, or rubbish from the mass media. Instead,

God's Spirit will lead me to expose myself to the finest in art, literature and music. He will put me in situations where my mind can be improved and my soul can be stimulated with that which is beautiful and noble and lofty. . .

"The same is true in the realm of my spirit, where I commune with Him. In the deep intuition of my innermost being where I 'know Him,' Christ comes to enlarge my life and the understanding of His will. He leads me to browse widely and ruminate richly in His Word. . . In short, because He does all this it is possible to make an impact on my generation out of all proportion to my one little life -- because He is in it with me." [1]

Spiritual Fitness

Utilizing a prioritized approach, let's begin with the immortal member of our being. Choosing to nourish our spirit with a healthy, daily diet of Bible study, prayer and quiet time with the Lord is akin to feeding the dog you wish to win every fight as in the above story.

"The survival of the fittest" law of nature applies to all aspects of life on this planet; spiritual, mental, emotional and physical. Alaskan bull moose males battle each fall for dominance in the mating season. Defeat is assured to one of the combatants when his antlers break. Invariably, the heftiest moose with the largest and strongest antlers is victorious and struts off with the females of the herd. The battle fought in the fall is won during the summer by the moose that consumes the best diet for gaining weight and growing antlers.

In a similar manner, successful living during the difficult days that lie ahead must be achieved now. God admonished Jeremiah of the present need to prepare for the perilous times of which the prophet was called to warn Judah. The Lord said to him, "If you have raced with men on foot and they have worn you out, how can you compete with horses? If you stumble in safe country, how will you manage in the thickets by the Jordan?" (Jeremiah 12:5).

A contemporary paraphrase of the above passage would be, "Stop moaning and groaning about your minor miseries, Jeremiah, because you ain't seen nothing yet. Get off your fanny and train for the heavyweight bout coming your way. If these small slaps wear you down, how will you withstand the heavy body blows soon to be thrown at you?

And if you lack the strength to deal well with the issues of life during this period of peace and prosperity, how will you perform with few goods and a loss of freedoms?"

Readiness Required

Even during times of peace and plenty, a crisis may occur in any of our lives without warning. And what's in us when it strikes is what will be revealed within our response to that situation. We fool ourselves when we assume there will be time to prepare for the unexpected.

Successful coaches know that unrelenting discipline, training and preparation are essential for establishing a long-term winning tradition. It won't just happen, and bursts of emotion can't substitute for their absence. The September 10th devotion in Oswald Chambers' My Utmost For His Highest stresses the need to be authentic before God at all times. He warns the reader against pretending to be and do as the Bible instructs, rather than working at it day-in and day-out. He encourages us to stop kidding ourselves in thinking we will rise to the occasion when a crisis occurs if we are not developing our character on a regular basis. That, he states, is what the Lord demands and expects of His children; and is the only way to truly worship our Creator. [2]

The early twentieth century "Apostle of Faith," Smith Wigglesworth, is quoted as having said the following: "Live ready. If you have to get ready when opportunity comes your way, you are too late. Opportunity does not wait, not even while you pray. You must not have to get ready; you must live ready."

A passage in the book of Joshua is, in my opinion, one of the more important Scriptures. Joshua 5:13-15 says, "Now when Joshua was near Jericho, he looked up and saw a man standing in front of him with a drawn sword in his hand. Joshua went up to him and asked, 'Are you for us or for our enemies?'

"'Neither,' he replied, 'but as commander of the army of the Lord, I have now come.' Then Joshua fell facedown to the ground in reverence, and asked him, 'What message does my Lord have for his servant?'

"The commander of the Lord's army replied, 'Take off your sandals, for the place where you are standing is holy.' And Joshua did so."

Joshua then received some most unorthodox instructions for conquering Jericho. He followed them explicitly and achieved a resounding victory.

Be On God's Side

Some believers try manipulating God into blessing their choices, actions and endeavors by obeying certain rules, rites and rituals, doing good deeds, or praying in a particular manner. They expect God to be for them and on their side; their agent so to speak. But the Creator of the universe requires us to be for Him and on His side.

We must learn, however, that He is faithful to those who fear, trust and obey Him. He is found by those who search for Him with all of their heart (Jeremiah 29:13). It's therefore vital that we reverence Him as King of kings and Lord of lords as did Joshua. And these are the essentials discovered by diligent and consistent study of God's Word. Application of the acquired knowledge within all aspects of our life must then follow.

I found the following excerpt of one of William Penn's many excellent writings in my file for such treasures. I don't recall the publication containing it, but want to share it with you. He wrote, "The unmortified Christian and the heathen are of the same religion, and the deity they truly worship is the god of this world. What shall we eat? What shall we drink? What shall we wear? And how shall we pass away our time? Which way may we gather and perpetuate our names and families in the earth? It is a mournful reflection, but a truth that will not be denied, that these worldly lusts fill up a great part of the study, care and conversation of Christendom. The false notion that they may be children of God while in a state of disobedience to His holy commandments, and disciples of Jesus though they revolt from His cross, and members of His true church, which is without spot or wrinkle, notwithstanding their lives are full of spots and wrinkles, is of all other deceptions upon themselves the most pernicious to their eternal condition for they are at peace in sin and under a security in their transgression."

It's fascinating to see that many who occupy pews in evangelical Christian churches at the start of the twenty-first century bear such a resemblance to those who did likewise over three hundred years ago. I suppose these great pretenders have always been there, and always will be to some extent. They can conceal their masquerade during times of peace and plenty, but difficult days unmask and expose us for what we are.

The prelude to the book of Jude (brother of Jesus) in The Open Bible attempts to awaken true disciples of Christ to the current dangers facing the Church. It says, "Fight! Contend! Do battle! When apostasy arises, when false teachers emerge, when the truth of God is attacked, it is time to fight for the faith. Only believers who are spiritually "in shape" can answer the summons. At the beginning of his letter Jude focuses on the believers' common salvation, but then feels compelled to challenge them to contend for the faith. The danger is real. False teachers have crept into the Church, turning God's grace into unbounded license to do as they please. Jude reminds such men of God's past dealings with unbelieving Israel, disobedient angels, and wicked Sodom and Gomorrah. In the face of such danger Christians should not be caught off guard. The challenge is great, but so is the God who is able to keep them from stumbling." [3]

As long as there's a daily need to feed your body to stay alive on this earth, I encourage you to do likewise to your spirit. Just as what we ate yesterday inadequately sustains us today, our prior study of God's Word and communication with Him has insufficient residual value. Daily quality time spent with our spouse and young children is required to maintain healthy and vibrant relationships with our loved ones. Why would it work any differently with our personal Lord and Savior, Jesus Christ?

Chapter Two Fitness of the Soul

It bears repeating. The soul is comprised of the mind, emotions and will. The mind makes all decisions which are enforced by the emotions and transacted by the will. The integration of these elements is so intense that, to some extent, they defy divisibility. Our thoughts influence our emotions, while at the same time are persuaded by them. And in a similar manner, our emotional state has a direct affect on our will; while its strength, or lack thereof, determines our emotional condition.

Mental Health

A tale from ancient India tells of four royal brothers who decided each to master a special ability. Time went by, and the brothers met to reveal what they had learned.

"I have mastered a science," said the first, "by which I can take but a bone of some creature and create the flesh that goes with it."

"I," said the second, "know how to grow that creature's skin and hair if there is flesh on its bones."

The third said, "I am able to create its limbs if I have the flesh, the skin, and the hair."

"And I," concluded the fourth, "know how to give life to that creature if its form is complete."

Thereupon the brothers went into the jungle to find a bone so they could demonstrate their specialties. As fate would have it, the bone they found was a lion's. One added flesh to the bone, the second grew hide and hair, the third completed it with matching limbs, and the fourth gave the lion life.
Shaking its mane, the ferocious beast arose and jumped on his creators. He killed them all and vanished contentedly into the jungle. *

So who says what we don't know can't hurt us? Lions in disguise lurk everywhere in this indulgent society awaiting to ambush unsuspecting believers in Christ. The internet has vastly increased the need for God-given discernment to distinguish between pertinent knowledge and mere information. The brilliant brothers in the above fable illustrate what destroys God's people as recorded in Hosea 4:6. Beyond the initial sentence stated earlier, the Lord says, "Because you have rejected knowledge, I also reject you as my priest; because you have ignored the law of your God, I also will ignore your children."

Centuries before the prophet Hosea walked the earth, King David knew the importance of biblical instruction. He says in Psalm 25, "Show me your ways, O Lord, teach me your paths; guide me in your truth and teach me, for you are God my Savior, and my hope is in you all day long. . . Good and upright is the Lord; therefore he instructs sinners in his ways. He guides the humble in what is right and teaches them his way. . . Who, then, is the man that fears the Lord? He will instruct him in the way chosen for him. He will spend his days in prosperity, and his descendants will inhabit the land."

Never before have good reading habits been more important for the moral health and well-being of followers of Christ. Beyond the daily study of Scripture, we need a steady diet of good teaching books, biographies of those used greatly of the Lord in ministry and secular endeavors in years past, and other quality literature that will challenge our thinking and expand our knowledge of good and evil. We must aggressively counter the moral rot and mind numbing nonsense with which the mass media fills the air waves and printed page.

We now know that good study habits benefit us physiologically as well as spiritually. An interesting and relevant article appeared in the Pittsburgh Post Gazette on July 30, 2000. The writer said, "The brain is like a muscle: Use it or lose it. That's the growing conclusion of research that shows fogged memory and slowed wit are not inevitable consequences of getting old, and there are steps people can take to protect their brains. . .

"'There are some things that, if you know you have a family history (of Alzheimer's) and you're just 20 to 30 years old, you can start doing to increase your protective factors,' said Dr. Amir Soas of Case Western Reserve University Medical School in Cleveland. . . 'Read, read, read . . . Anything that stimulates the brain to think,' he said.

"And cut back on TV, Soas insists. 'When you watch television, your brain goes into neutral,' he said. So much so that Case Western plans to study whether people who contract Alzheimer's watched more TV throughout life than healthy seniors. . .

"Case Western scientists studied 550 people and found those less mentally and physically active in middle age were three times more likely to get Alzheimer's as they grayed. Particularly protective: increasing intellectual activity during adulthood." [4]

Selective Study Essential

I agree with Dr. Soas about the importance of reading; but carefully choosing what to read is equally valid. Both spiritual and psychological health is preserved when we guard against the prevalent six "isms". Humanism tells us that man is the highest authority in the universe; the master of his own destiny; and is justified in doing whatever his circumstances dictate since there is no superior power to which he should appeal. Materialism proclaims that our possessions and achievements, not our character, is what measures our self worth and inner fulfillment. And Scientism attempts to convince us that all which is real or pertinent must be examined and evaluated on the basis of our five physical senses; giving no relevance to that which is of a spiritual dimension.

Atheism claims that all which exists occurred by chance in an evolutionary manner; without purpose, meaning or direction since there is no actuality of a supreme being who influences life on this planet. Religionism, on the other hand, professes the existence of God, but defines His character and conduct through the dark, debased and distorted viewpoint of unregenerate man. And Spiritism encourages us to make contact with the spiritual realm through all forms of demonism and satanic emulation; encompassing all that is within the occult.

Many destructive forces, both natural and supernatural, exert themselves against us in an unrelenting manner. We won't just happen to resist or repel them, or even recognize them for that matter. It requires a persistent and dedicated effort to daily feed our mind with what is of God, and thus what is for our ultimate good. Only then can we heed Paul's advice found in Philippians 4:8. He said, "Finally, brothers, whatever is pure, whatever is lovely, whatever is admirable -- if anything is excellent or praiseworthy -- think about such things."

Mental Health Conclusion

I want to conclude this segment with three quotes. The first is by the brilliant Jewish radio talk show host, Dennis Prager. He said, "One thing I noticed about Evangelicals is that they don't read. They do not read the Bible, they do not read the great Christian thinkers, they have never heard of Aquinas. If they're Presbyterian, they've never read the founders of Presbyterianism. I do not understand this. As a Jew, that's confusing to me. The commandment of study is so deep in Judaism that we immerse ourselves in study. God gave us a brain, aren't we to use it for His service?" [5] He goes on to say that, as a Jew, he owns far more Christian books than do most Christians. Of the many long-term believers I have known, few maintain healthy reading habits. And those who don't, give themselves little chance of gaining a strong grasp of Scripture with the ability to practically apply it to all areas of their lives.

The second quote is from Pastor Kent Hughes who said, "I have great sympathy for those whose past has been a series of bad choices. I understand that if over the years one has chosen the impure and the illusory and the negative, it is very difficult to change. But as a Biblical thinker I give no quarter to myself or anyone else who rationalizes his present choices by the past. Brothers, as Christians we are free to have a Christian mind. It is within our reach, and it is our duty." [6]

The last quote is the Open Bible's translation of the first part of Proverbs 19:2. King Solomon said, "Also it is not good for a soul to be without knowledge." [3]

Chapter Three Emotional Security and Stability

A *certain Irishman stayed* too long at the pub one evening. On the way home, as his car weaved side to side on a deserted road, a cop pulled him over and asked where he had been.

"Why, I've been to the pub of course," slurred the drunk.

"It would appear you 'ad a bit too much to drink before driving 'ome," said the officer.

"That I did," admitted the lush with a smile.

"Did you know now that a few intersections back your wife fell out of the car?," asked the policeman.

"Oh, thanks be to the Lord," sighed the drunk. "I was fearing I 'ad gone deaf."

Not long after that, his lovely wife, Mary Clancy, went up to speak with Father O'Grady after his Sunday morning service. Seeing the tears running down her cheeks, he said, "So what would be bothering you my child?"

She answered, "Oh, Father, I've got terrible news. My husband passed away last night."

The priest replied, "Oh, Mary, I am so very sorry for your loss. Tell me, my dear, did 'e 'ave any last request?"

"Aye, that he did," responded the grieving spouse.

"What might that 'ave been?," asked the Reverend O'Grady.

"He said, 'Please Mary my dearest, put the darn gun down,'" she answered.

The condition of our key relationships is both a reflection of and influence on our emotional state. It doesn't take a nuclear physicist to diagnose the Clancy marital union as being unfit. Such an obvious degree of unrest within the home, even had Mary honored her husband's final request, would adversely impact all aspects of their lives.

First Things First

A vibrant relationship with our Lord and Savior Jesus Christ is the corner stone upon which strong marriages, healthy parent-child relationships, and overall emotional security and stability is built. Nothing on this earth during my brief stay here can erode my foundation when it's composed of trusting in Almighty God, relying on the veracity of His Word, obeying it, and resting in His faithfulness.

The psalmist said, "He who dwells in the shelter of the Most High will rest in the shadow of the Almighty. . . If you will make the Most High your dwelling -- even the Lord who is my refuge -- then no harm will befall you, no disaster will come near your tent. For he will command his angels concerning you to guard you in all your ways. . .'Because he loves me,' says the Lord, 'I will rescue him; I will protect him, for he acknowledges my name. He will call upon me, and I will answer him; I will be with him in trouble, I will deliver him and honor him. With long life will I satisfy him and show him my salvation'" (Psalm 91:1,9-11,14-16).

Unsuitable Substitutes

How does that match up with some of the more prevalent substitutes such as trusting in others, scientific advancements, wealth, position, accomplishments or winning the lottery? All of these are fleeting, unreliable, unfulfilling and incapable of meeting our innermost needs, hopes and expectations. It's obvious, however, that man's nature intuitively relies on that which he thinks he can physically grasp, use and control to lead him safely and successfully throughout his pilgrimage on this cold and impersonal planet.

Strangely enough, a recent article in the New York Times reveals that many modern day folks attach themselves to something over which they can exercise no ownership or control in their search for happiness and contentment. The writer said, "It has long been assumed that ardent sports fans derive excitement and a sense of community from rooting for a big-time team. But a growing body of scientific evidence suggests that, for some fans, the ties go much deeper.

"Some researchers have found that fervent fans get so tied to their teams that they experience hormonal surges and other physiological changes while watching games, much as the athletes themselves do.

"The self-esteem of some male and female fans also rises and fall with the outcome, with losses affecting their optimism about everything from getting a date to playing darts, one study showed." [7]

Researchers conclude that forming such deep ties to sports teams for which they do not play, coach, work or own is somewhat good for their health. They say it provides enjoyment and something to hope in, but also express that science is still grappling with many questions regarding this subject.

As a lifetime athlete and sports junkie, I have no problem with the enjoyment aspect. But my hope requires something far more stable and secure than the fickle fortunes of athletic contests. Let's recall, however, that science only examines and evaluates what can be experienced by the five physical senses; concluding that nothing beyond that exists. Therefore the only factors considered are those which are temporal and precarious.

It troubles me that those who do not personally know or submit to the Creator of this universe, He Who installed and supports its very pillars, must cling to and depend upon some element of His creation. Even the thinking and comprehension of those with gifted intellects are limited to material substance.

It disturbs me further that many who have experienced the reality of the living Christ refuse to allow His Holy Spirit to open their eyes to what exists beyond the three dimensional physical realm. It's only in this fourth dimension that we find that which is faithful and true, unchanging and eternal. But achieving true and lasting peace and contentment compels us to release all that we have been fervently clutching. And that's a major sticking point for countless born-again believers.

Simplification Required

In his Testament of Devotion, Thomas Kelly said, "We feel honestly the pull of many obligations and try to fulfill them all. And we are unhappy, uneasy, strained, oppressed, and fearful we shall be shallow." But then he provides hope and promise when he says, "We have hints that there is a way of life vastly richer and deeper than all this hurried existence, a life of unhurried serenity and peace and power. If only we could skip over into that Center!" [8]

Richard Foster, author of the excellent Freedom Of Simplicity, says it this way: "Within all of us is a whole conglomerate of selves. . . Each one screams to protect his or her vested interests. . . But when we experience life at the Center, all is changed. Our many selves come under the unifying control of the divine Arbitrator. No longer are we forced to live by an inner majority rule which always leaves a disgruntled minority." [9]

Both of these serious Bible students learned that we really can hear God in such a way that each decision can be ordered and governed by Him.

But such a way of living is far from automatic, simply by willing it to be so. We are creatures of habit, and our present style of frantic-paced living and divided allegiance will not bow out without a good fight. We must sincerely desire for Christ to Man the center of our wills; and we must seek it out. We must have a strong working knowledge and understanding of the basic principles of God's Word, and strive daily to order our lives in accordance with it. Only such a consciously chosen course of action will draw us more deeply into perpetual communion with the Father. Much effort and practice is required.

And finally, we must refuse to live beyond our means emotionally. This requires us to get the broad picture on the events of our time and evaluate them. This is called "existence clarification" -- whereby we perceive what is happening in modern society, see where it will lead us, then live one day at a time in harmony with God's plan and purpose for our lives. Paradoxically, we simply cannot use an emotional approach for achieving emotional security and stability.

Chapter Four Reconciling Our Will with God's Will

The major debate between various Protestant denominations concerns the Supremacy of God and Man's Free-will. The Calvinists insist that only those who God pre-chose (the Elect) are saved, and the Lord orders and controls every aspect of their lives. The Arminians, on the other hand, teach that our free-will choices determine whether or not we accept Jesus as Lord and Savior, and if we persevere or lose our Salvation along the way. The Bible explicitly teaches both. The truth, therefore, is that God orders everything in our lives while we are free to choose to obey or disobey His commands and instructions. This is a paradox (an apparent but not real contradiction) that our finite minds cannot reconcile.

We must ask the Lord for the courage to stand in the tension between these two extremes rather than submitting to our fear of the unknown and unknowable. The Bible doesn't permit us to delete segments with which we don't agree or understand. Thus we can't accept one of these positions and dismiss the other.

A large portion of Scripture would be unnecessary if we did not have a free will. Countless Old and New Testament passages strongly encourage us to make wise and wholesome choices based on God's way of life and living. Many others admonish us for abiding in a manner that leads us away from Him; and tells of the inevitable consequences of continuing to do so.

On the other hand, the Bible wouldn't exist if God didn't have a master plan for man's existence; and the power and purpose to bring it about. The Old Testament is a consistent and progressive historic account of that plan from the creation of the universe to a few centuries prior to the birth of Christ. Most biblical prophecy has been precisely fulfilled over the past two thousand years, and that which remains is readily possible.

I believe that it's essential for all Christians to take seriously their responsibility for knowing and doing God's will in all aspects of their lives. I don't understand, nor need to, where the boundaries of my free-will choices and God's intervention converge within the numerous and diverse situations encountered in life. It seems from my personal experiences and observation of others that those boundaries are determined, to a large degree, by the extent of my desire and willingness to submit all things to the Lord.

Evidence Of Their Co-Existence

The lives of believers are a curious blend of man's free will and God's supremacy. Many travel the "Path of Least Resistance" until it takes them where they don't want to go. Only then does it become clear that they either make a radical change in how they think and act, or slip over the edge of the cliff just two steps before them. Their backs must be against the wall before they are willing to exercise discipline and self-denial. And while God didn't cause them to sin and bring them to that hard place, it's obvious that He allowed them to come where He finally had their attention.

Conversely, there are those who have consistently obeyed the Lord and still found themselves in difficult circumstances. Their lives resemble the story of Joseph as told in the book of Genesis. Even though he was being obedient to his father, he still ended up in a pit. And for the next few years of his life, he was either toiling as a slave or languishing in prison. But because he refused to blame or disobey God during his hard times, he miraculously rose from the dungeon to become the second most powerful man in Egypt. This then empowered him to use his position and influence to save his father's entire family which was called by God to form the twelve tribes of Israel.

Joseph's incredible story is summed up near the end of the final chapter of Genesis. He said to his brothers who feared his retribution after their father died, "You intended to harm me, but God intended it for good to accomplish what is now being done, the saving of many lives" (Genesis 50:20).

The purpose of this book is to awaken the reader to realize that he or she is the one that must determine the direction their life will take from the place in which they now find themselves. A healthy and alert mind is required to understand what brought them here; and how to reverse their course, or proceed in their current manner based on their existing condition. They then must stabilize or preserve their emotional state in accordance with faith in the Lord and trust in His promises. And finally, they must act in bringing their own will into conformity with His.

Discipline Has No Alternative

An excellent illustration of that which I speak occurred at Valley Forge during the winter and early spring of 1778. While the soldiers were enduring horrendous hardships and struggling just to survive, George Washington was intent on creating a disciplined fighting force for the upcoming offensive. He assigned the task of converting this ragged bunch of Continentals into a professional army to a volunteer named Friedrich Wilhelm Augustus Baron von Steuben.

This man was a much decorated former captain in the Prussian army, and staff officer of Frederick the Great. He came highly recommended by Ben Franklin, and had a passion for drill. He created a drill manual for the colonists, then worked tirelessly at training the various companies of soldiers. He drilled them incessantly in the many steps to firing a musket. By the time spring came, each company could produce a crisp volley of musket balls every fifteen seconds. By April, the Continental Army was thinking, marching and acting as one. All of their maneuvers were crisp and precise.

The exhausted and near-defeated band of undisciplined fighters that entered Valley Forge on December 19, 1777, were now a confident military force with high morale ready to take on the world's most powerful army. Washington knew all too well that simply enduring and surviving a hard time would in no way prepare them for the difficult task that awaited them. If he didn't totally change their way of thinking, responding to orders and carrying out his commands, they would soon regret having survived that horrible winter. (10)

It's important to realize that hard times alone don't change people. In fact, if they refuse to toil relentlessly at altering everything within their power relative to that which brought their trials upon them, their circumstances will only deteriorate. Aside from Joshua and Caleb, all of the Israelites over the age of 21 who marched out of their Egyptian slavery died in the wilderness. The Bible tells us they continued to think and act as those in bondage, rather than transforming their minds into believers who recognize, celebrate and behave as those whom the Lord has set free. God could not permit them to enter Canaan, because that mindset would prevent them from standing up to and defeating the seven strong nations inhabiting that land. They would quickly return to bondage, and it would be far worse than it was in Egypt. Not only would the temperament and customs of the people be unfamiliar, but they would pay dearly for attempting to take their land.

Let's say it one more time. All decisions are made in our mind, enforced by our emotions and transacted by our will. If we are to be fully prepared for whatever may lie ahead, we must both know and do as God instructs in His Word.

Physical Fitness

This topic requires its own chapter, and that is what follows.

Lesson Two
Importance of Physical Fitness

I HAVE DECIDED TO DEVOTE an entire lesson to this subject since it is generally ignored or avoided within the Christian community. Most preaching from the pulpit involves spiritual issues which of course is right and proper. And the elements of our soul seem to generate their share of attention in church since study, behavior and relationships are a substantial part of a righteous life.

It bothers me, however, that one third of our total being is essentially excluded from the Christian experience. You would think that our three components were independent and segregated from one another. That just isn't reality as previously illustrated. So let's try to balance the room with the following information.

A fair portion of my physiology knowledge was derived from a wonderful book entitled Your Body, His Temple. Dr. A. L. Heller wrote it around 1980, and supported its contents with proper use of a generous portion of Scripture. [1] It has, unfortunately, been out of print for many years. That's a testimony to the lack of interest in our physical well-being by Bible-believing Christians.

Pastor Bill Hybels shares my frustration with the Church's disregard for the proper maintenance of what the Bible defines as the temple of the Holy Spirit. In his excellent Honest To God?, he says, "If caring for our bodies were nothing more than an act of vanity, I wouldn't waste a lesson on it. If I were convinced that God is only concerned with our souls (spirits), I would join the majority of Christians who neglect this subject. But Scripture clearly reveals God's concern about our physical well-being.

"The human body is no fluke of evolution's process. It is God's design and handiwork. It is His masterpiece. It is the ultimate synthesis between function and beauty. Our most advanced technology pales in comparison to the capabilities of the human body. . . So caring for our bodies is a responsibility we owe to God." [2]

The Great Commission commands us to "Therefore go and make disciples of all nations, baptizing them in the name of the Father and of the Son and of the Holy Spirit, and teaching them to obey everything I have commanded you" (Matthew 28:19,20). To what extent has this task been hindered by disciples of Christ with healthy spirits, knowledgeable minds, submissive wills but sick and weak bodies?

Chapter Five A False Concept

God did not create the "Planned Obsolescence" postulate. That was the no-brainer-child instituted around 1960 by one or more of America's large manufacturers. World War II had been over for fifteen years, and the country was enjoying a degree of prosperity. Man's greed, however, was back in full swing as evidenced by the intentional use of inferior materials to limit their product's useful life. The plan, of course, was to assure the consumer's need to replace it before too long.

That is not the way God created our bodies. Nothing that man has invented compares with its complexity, durability, practicality, adaptability, style, capacity for work and reproductive ability. Aside from unavoidable defects, injuries and illness, it is capable of functioning efficiently during our entire sojourn on this earth. A loving and compassionate God wouldn't put us here for sixty, seventy, eighty or more years in a vehicle not built to make the whole trip.

But it doesn't just happen. We are obligated to understand its needs and care for it diligently throughout our life. Recognizing the dangers our twenty-first century affluent and indulgent culture poses to our physical well-being, we are held accountable for what we feed it, how we use it, the activities and involvements in which we permit it to participate, and the amount of rest given it.

The Heart

An accurate definition of physical fitness is having a strong heart, strong lungs and strong blood vessels. The seven components contributing to being fit are proper weight, a healthy diet, regular aerobic and weight-resistant exercise, adequate sleep, abstinence from all habit-forming drugs including nicotine, stress management and periodic physical examinations.

Our body, as described above, is the engineering masterpiece that houses our spirit and soul. Since we are dealing with the essence of good stewardship, let's get right to the heart of the matter.

I'm referring to the 4-chambered, muscular pump that moves over 4,000 gallons of blood per day through 75,000 miles of blood vessels. Yes, you heard that right. I don't recommend you try it, but if you took out all of your arteries, veins and capillaries and laid them end-to-end, they would go coast to coast and back again almost a dozen times.

The heart beats over 100,000 times per day, and 36 1/2 million times per year. Each of those is a contraction of the thick muscle of the heart wall to force the blood into circulation. It then relaxes and refills with returning blood. The sole purpose of the blood's extensive travels is to supply each of our seven trillion cells with oxygen and nutrients, and remove from them carbon dioxide and other waste products. Imagine what happens to various parts of our body when a weak and atrophied heart muscle disrupts the duties of the supply truck and waste haulers.

King Solomon said, "Above all else, guard your heart, for it is the wellspring of life" (Proverbs 4:23). He of course was speaking of our spirit, the innermost part of our being. But the muscular blood pump defined above serves a parallel purpose relative to our physical existence on earth.

I recall watching the 700 Club late in February of 1976. A guest on the show was a young Christian man who operated a fitness club in the south. He spoke about the structure and function of the heart, and the essential need to exercise it regularly. Along with supplying blood to all the cells, a strong heart and healthy blood vessels provide oxygen to the brain and muscles throughout the body. An adequate supply of such is vital for their efficient operation.

The young man said, "Many middle-aged people leave their homes each day with less than a full tank of oxygen to perform a task requiring one. If you call your attorney mid-afternoon and hear him yawning on the other end of the line, it's a safe bet he has exhausted his supply of oxygen for that day. He is, at that point, incapable of thinking clearly and providing the professional guidance you may need. It would be best to call back the next morning."

I was thirty-three at the time, and ready to admit that my physical conditioning was at an all-time low. Time availability for athletic involvement had declined significantly, and my playing skills suffered accordingly. The 700 Club guest gave me a wake-up call. He helped me understand why I felt lethargic much of the time; and why it was becoming more difficult to keep up with my high-energy young children. I respond best when my comprehension is enlightened, so I was jogging on the local track the next day.

Despite multiple knee surgeries since then, I've maintained a healthy degree of cardiovascular fitness. My energy level remains high, and I continue in various physical involvements. My reading habits have likewise progressed, since the ability to think clearly and retain the knowledge acquired expanded accordingly. This in turn has improved my walk with the Lord, and thus the intense integration of the three components of my being has been most evident.

The 7/30/2000 Pittsburgh Post Gazette article referenced in the previous chapter concurred with my personal experience. It read in part, "People have to get physical too. Bad memory is linked to heart disease, diabetes and a high-fat diet, all risks people can counter by living healthier lives. In fact, provocative new research suggests these brain-protective steps, mental and physical, may be strong enough to help influence who gets Alzheimer's disease. . .

"But physical health is important, too. A healthy brain needs lots of oxygen pumped through healthy arteries. Haan (lead researcher Mary Haan of the University of Michigan) studied people who have a gene called ApoE4, which significantly increases the risk of Alzheimer's. Brain function of gene carriers declined four times faster with age if they also had hardened arteries or diabetes. High-fat diets increased the risk seven times, Case Western researchers found. That means exercising and eating right -- the very things that prevent heart disease and diabetes -- helps the brain, too." [3]

Proper Weight

The owner of the physical fitness establishment, interviewed on the 2/27/76 edition of the 700 Club, discussed the disgusting term obesity. While significantly overweight folks always qualify, so do some who don't carry extra pounds. He stated that a particular one hundred and ten pound homemaker in her thirties who tested at his club for body fat, met the criteria which classified her as obese.

The American Medical Association Home Medical Encyclopedia defines obesity as "A condition in which there is too much body fat. Being obese is not the same as being overweight." But since the two are often thought to be synonymous and are certainly related, one is generally not considered to be obese unless he or she weighs twenty percent or more over the maximum desirable weight for his or her height.

The AMA encyclopedia goes on to say, "It is estimated that about 25 percent of the U.S. population carries too much fat. About 5 to 10 percent of children are overweight or obese. Between 13 and 23 percent of all adolescents (especially girls) are obese; 80 percent of obese teenagers are likely to grow into obese adults."

It states that obese people do not always eat considerately more than thin people. One's metabolic rate (the amount of energy required to maintain vital body functions at rest) , activity level and calorie intake are the key factors here. Although a complex issue, a simple formula applies. Obesity occurs when calories consumed exceed calories expended.

"Obesity increases a person's chance of becoming seriously ill." High blood pressure, stroke, coronary heart disease, adult-onset diabetes, various types of cancer, osteoarthritis and joint malfunction are all significantly more prevalent in obese people according to the American Medical Association. The risk of all of those increase proportionately with the degree and duration of obesity. [4]

Proper weight is therefore the correct number of pounds per inch of height in accordance with one's bone structure. Charts are available to help you determine your ultimate weight, but it seems that most adults know the poundage at which they look, feel and function their best. Once the ultimate weight is achieved, consistent exercise is necessary to remove and/or keep excess fat from accumulating within the muscle mass.

Considering what you now know about the basic function of the heart, permit me to give you an added incentive to prevent or terminate obesity. Medical scientists estimate that an additional 4,000 feet of blood vessels are required for supplying nourishment to each additional pound of fat carried. That poor old blood pump has a gruelling around-the-clock task to perform under ultimate conditions. It's best not to make it tougher.

A Healthy Diet

The great detective Sherlock Holmes and his faithful sidekick, Dr. Watson, went on a wilderness camping trip. After a good meal and a bottle of wine, they entered their tent and went to sleep. Some hours later, Holmes awoke and nudged his faithful friend. "Watson, look up at the sky and tell me what you see." Watson replied, "I see millions and millions of stars."

"What does that tell you?," asked Holmes.

Watson pondered the question for a minute, then answered, "Astronomically, it tells me that there are millions of galaxies and potentially billions of planets. Astrologically, I observe that Saturn is in Leo. Horologically, I deduce that it is approximately 3:30 A.M. Theologically, I can see that God is all-powerful and we are but small and insignificant. Meteorologically, I suspect that we will have a beautiful day tomorrow.

What does it tell you?"

Holmes was silent for a moment, then said, "Watson, you idiot. It means someone has stolen our tent!"

This reminds me of those brilliant folks who spend a fortune on a good education, then work sixty hours a week for the next twenty-five years pursuing their chosen career. Maintaining that frantic pace requires them to skip meals on occasion, and feast on high saturated fat junk food most other times. Salt and sugar loaded snacks are also consumed in large quantities to ease the pressure and tedium of their days. When they finally stop to enjoy a good meal, they devour a huge cholesterol pervaded steak, and wash it down with too much alcohol.

Just when it's time to enjoy the fruit of their labor, the wheels come off and their engine implodes. They confirm the wisdom of the sage who said, "Men will lose their health to acquire wealth; then spend all they have in an effort to regain

41

it." Like Dr. Watson, their obsession with complex matters obscures the obvious. Misusing, abusing and neglecting the vehicle in which their life-long journey must be made has failure, frustration and foolishness written all over it.

No extensive dialogue on maintaining a healthy diet is forthcoming. That is a distinct and complex study all by itself. Dr. A.L. Heller said, "The basis for a successful program of getting unwanted body fat off and keeping it off is a combination of exercise and restriction of food intake. . . It is eating foods that still satisfy your desire for food while not overloading the body with calories. In short, it is not willpower needed but knowledge of how to select natural foods and then prepare these foods properly. God can change our desire for food, but it is our responsibility to learn about food and its nutritional value. . .

"Preparing good food that is not fattening depends on knowing which foods contain the most calories. Make no mistake about it--calories do count. It doesn't make any difference whether a calorie is in a protein food, a fat food, or a carbohydrate food. A calorie is a calorie and it is a unit of energy. Remember that energy can neither be created nor destroyed. If you swallow and absorb a calorie, your body must process it. You will use it for energy or store it as fat." [5]

Only a fool puts cheap fuel in an expensive automobile which is created by man, and depended upon for many aspects of our day-to-day life. So how irresponsible is it to put junk foods in God's engineering marvel which He created, bought and dwells in?

A high-sugar diet causes ailments as diverse as heart disease, diabetes, obesity, mood swings and tooth decay. A high-saturated fat diet clogs up the arteries causing high blood pressure and related diseases; as well as certain types of cancer. A high-salt diet contributes to high blood pressure, fluid retention, digestive complications, and a host of other problems. The New American Diet cookbook by Sonia L. Connor, M.S., R.D., and William E. Connor, M.D., published by Simon and Schuster, is recommended reading since God made our bodies to function properly on pure, natural foods. It outlines a gradual, four-phase transition from victuals that damage the body to nutritious eating.

Regular Exercise

The average American lifestyle over the past forty or so years bears little resemblance to that of most humans throughout mankind's history. Hard physical labor and travel by foot or upon animals has generally been the norm. Knowing that would be the case, the Creator fashioned our bodies to function best when vigorously used in a consistent manner. The way most contemporary Americans make their living and spend their leisure time is therefore detrimental to their physical well-being. Considerable more movement and external resistance is needed in most cases for achieving optimal health and a state of readiness for answering God's call.

Proper and adequate exercise can be attained in a variety of ways. Each activity, however, must fall into one of two general categories to be beneficial. The first, aerobic exercise, is that which "is vigorous enough to tax the power of the muscles and should be done long enough and strenuously enough to produce a sense of healthy fatigue." [6] Aerobic exercise increases oxygen consumption by demanding a steady output from your muscles over an extended period of time. Cardiovascular benefit is achieved when a pulse rate of around seventy-five percent of maximum is maintained for at least twenty minutes. Examples are jogging, swimming, cycling, brisk walking, and sports such as basketball, hockey, tennis and racquetball. Running at the mouth or playing the radio don't qualify.

Weight training is exercise that uses resistance for building and maintaining muscle mass. This is achieved in a variety of ways, but generally requires some type of equipment or device. There are several exercises, however, that utilize one's own body weight for an adequate weight training workout. Picking up hitchhikers or resisting arrest doesn't qualify for this category.

The ideal conditioning program is a consistent blend of the two types of exercise. But if you're inclined to just do one of them, or can only make time for one, let it be aerobic. Cardiovascular exercise is most important since it strengthens the heart, maintains healthy blood vessels, and provides the necessary blood flow through the body as well as an adequate supply of oxygen-carrying hemoglobin in the blood. The ability of the muscle cells to process the oxygen and eliminate wastes is likewise enhanced, and as a result the heart is not forced to overwork.

Aerobic exercise also expands the working space and efficiency of your lungs, and increases the number of tiny blood vessels that form a network throughout the cells of your body. It's one of the best cures for obesity and substantially improves mental alertness.

Weight training builds and maintains muscle mass which is important to your overall health and energy level. Strong and vibrant muscles protect the bones, improve posture and present a pleasing appearance. But perhaps their greatest benefit is the manner in which they assist the metabolic process.

Metabolism is the body's ability to breakdown the food consumed and convert it into energy. It occurs within the muscles which are the body's energy cells. Operating at peak efficiency, this process separates the food into its various components, introduces them into the blood stream, and ships them out as nourishment to our seven trillion cells. When our muscle mass is infiltrated with fat, both the separation and delivery procedures are inefficiently performed. As a result, the energy locked in food is not fully released, and unused calories are stored as additional fat. Weight training therefore speeds up weight loss by increasing muscle mass and burning more calories at rest.

If you can find no other motivation to initiate and maintain a good exercise program, do it so you can eat well without gaining weight.

Adequate Sleep

It is wise to shut down an expensive and important machine when friction causes it to heat up. On the other hand, engines and moving parts need to be used regularly to prevent rust and corrosion, and operate at peak efficiency. The elements of this planet attack that which is used too much, too little or carelessly. Our bodies which are machines in the truest sense function under the same principles. We spoke above of the need to exercise them in a sufficient and consistent manner. We must now discuss our need for adequate sleep.

The insatiable "Get all you can, can all you get, and sit on the can" materialistic compulsion is often the cause of people getting insufficient sleep. It creates such a complexity of demands and desires, time just isn't available for what is needed. But sometimes the crush of legitimate responsibilities keeps a person going too many hours each twenty-four hour day. In either case, a prudent individual must replace the urgent with the important if he/she wishes to remain productive. Those who continue to ignore this vital necessity are often involuntarily removed from the action for an extended period of time.

Couch potatoes reside on the opposite end of the spectrum. They misuse and abuse their physical and mental capacities by wasting the precious life God gave them. Too much rest causes the heart and other muscles to atrophy, replacing them with excessive and destructive body fat. Clear thinking and creative expression are likewise lost when an inactive cardiovascular system supplies insufficient oxygen to the brain. Depression and apathy generally result, with an explosion of some type required to get these folks moving.

The first group needs to revisit the Mount and hear Jesus say, "Do not store up for yourself treasures on earth, where moth and rust destroy, and where thieves break in and steal. But store up for yourselves treasures in heaven. . . For where your treasure is, there your heart will be also. . . So do not worry, saying, 'What shall we eat?' or 'What shall we drink?' or 'What shall we wear?'. . . But seek first his kingdom and his righteousness, and all these things will be given to you as well" (Matthew 6:19-21,31,33).

Group B should sit down with wise King Solomon and listen to him expound on those who expend little energy in living their gift of life. He says, "How long will you lie there, you sluggard? When will you get up from your sleep? A little sleep, a little slumber, a little folding of the hands to rest--and poverty will come on you like a bandit and scarcity like an armed man" (Proverbs 6:9-11).

Abstain From Habit Forming Drugs

Dr. A.L. Heller said this about smoking: "The American Lung Association informs us that smoke from tobacco contains over 500 known poisons. Among them are carbon monoxide, hydrogen cyanide (a respiratory enzyme poison), pyridine, phenols (cancer-causing agents), aldehydes that irritate the lungs, acrolein (World War I gas), and many hydrocarbons. This smoke (and its accompanying poisons) is absorbed by your lips, oral cavity, and esophagus, and is drawn deep into your lungs. Nicotine irritates the stomach and intestines when swallowed and irritates lung tissue when inhaled.

"The carbon monoxide in the smoke, like that coming out of automobile exhaust, lowers your red blood cells' capability of carrying oxygen. Red blood cells can carry either oxygen or carbon monoxide, and the monoxide gets first preference. . . Nicotine in cigarette smoke increases heart rate as much as 25 beats per minute, makes blood more likely to clot, and constricts blood vessels--all making the heart work harder to get blood through the vessels. If our heart has to work harder for a habit, does it seem logical to waste extra beats that could be put to better use health wise?" [7]

All habit forming drugs alter the normal rhythm of the heart by introducing foreign chemicals into the blood stream. Over time, damaging side effects will far exceed the momentary pleasure of the "high" they produce.

Chapter Six Managing Stress

Since God placed us in this pleasure-seeking society, why not partake of what is labelled "runner's high?" Many who jog regularly and experience this delightful feeling afterwards, believe it's simply a psychological reward for doing what's best for their physical well-being. But it's far more. An extended period of maintaining their pulse rate at around seventy five percent of maximum produces what is termed vasodilatation. This is the enlargement of the blood vessels through which travels an increased supply of oxygen-enriched blood to the brain and muscles having an antidepressant effect. Vigorous exercise also causes the pituitary gland to release the powerful hormone endorphin into the bloodstream. Endorphin, the body's natural painkiller, produces increased energy, an improved attitude, a mood balance, and a general sense of well-being. [8]

Simplifying your life and being content with what God has given you is a major step towards stress reduction. Much tension and worry accompanies the extensive process of gaining more wealth, things and status. Then additional stress is created by the effort required to maintain and retain all that's secured.

The happiest people I've known are those who appreciate life's simple pleasures.

They dwell on the known and knowable, trusting the Lord to shield them and their loved ones from what they can't comprehend nor control. They permit the truth of Scripture and promises of their Savior to illuminate their path and perspective. They perform their tasks, honor their commitments, and fulfill their responsibilities. They focus on who they are and what they have, refusing to desire what can't rightfully be obtained. They take their stand upon the duty of the hour, thus avoiding the pain of regret.

At least much, often most, and sometimes all stress is produced by our manner of thinking and responding to conditions, circumstances and contemporaries. We blame others, curse our state of affairs, and bemoan the realities of life. But nothing changes unless and until the burden of achieving our own peace and serenity essential for our physical well-being is personally accepted.

Stress management is most efficiently achieved by he or she who is always calm, gentle and patient. Treating others with courtesy and compassion is the best thing one can do for himself relative to interpersonal relationships. The manner in which others treat us is seldom much different than how we greeted or responded to them. When I look intently at what is said and done to me, I see but a reflection of what I have said and done to others.

Stress is successfully and consistently managed only by those who remain superior to their possessions, physical and mental attributes, circumstances, environment, and the opinions and attitudes of others. They strive only for virtue since it alone is permanent; and spend all they have on developing character, as it alone is essential.

Stress reduction is simply a by-product of living in accordance with instructions found in the Gospels. When we seek first the kingdom of God and His righteousness, all the things we fret about, fuss over and frantically pursue is added to us. They may look different than what we thought we wanted, but we shall find they are all that we need. And as a bonus, we now have the health and energy to enjoy them.

Periodic Physical Examinations

Your body is an engineering masterpiece of design and function. Be wise and take it to the shop now and again for repairs, routine maintenance and safety inspections.

Establishing Priorities

A preacher stood before his congregation and filled a large jar with rocks. He asked the worshippers if they considered the jar to be full, and they agreed that it was.

He then poured in a box of pebbles that filled the crevices between the rocks. Once again he asked the listeners if they thought the jar was full. With a chuckle they agreed that it was.

He then poured in some sand that filled the cavities between the pebbles, and with a smile announced that the jar was finally filled. He said, "Think of it as your life. The rocks are its important components such as your relationships with the Lord, your spouse and your children; and your mental, emotional and physical well-being. The loss of any of these greatly impacts your life in a negative manner.

"The pebbles are things such as your job, house, cars, ministry involvement and social activities. These are important, but replaceable. The sand is everything else that receives some time, energy or resources. These are enjoyable, but by no means essential."

The preacher then emptied the jar and put the pebbles and sand back in first. Now there was insufficient room for all the rocks. The message was clear: "Put first things first, giving all which has purpose and meaning the time and attention they need and deserve; because all else is just pebbles and sand."

Lesson Three
The Foundation of Faith

PERFECT SPIRIT, SOUL AND BODY fitness is not possible during our temporal existence. But consistent and persistent growth and development until we go home to the Lord and be perfect as He is perfect should be our goal. It's possible and achieved only by adding layer upon layer to our character. This process is best defined by 2 Peter 1:5-7 that instructs us to add goodness, knowledge, self-control, perseverance, godliness, brotherly kindness and love to our faith, in that order.

It is comprehensible how to add something of substance to that which already exists. But how do we define and create the foundation upon which all else rests when there appears to be nothing from which it evolves or of which it consists? How important is faith? How much effort should be expended in developing a deep-rooted trust in God and His Word?

The Bible says, "Now faith is being sure of what we hope for and certain of what we do not see. This is what the ancients were commended for. By faith we understand that the universe was formed at God's command, so that what is seen was not made out of what was visible. . . And without faith it is impossible to please God, because anyone who comes to him must believe that he exists and that he rewards those who earnestly seek him" (Hebrews 11:1,2,3 & 6).

With that said, most of this lesson will be concerned with answering the first of the above three questions. It's not possible to improve upon the response to the latter two questions provided by the Hebrews passage, so no effort will be wasted thereon.

Chapter Seven Faith Defined

Webster defines faith as "belief or trust that does not question or ask for proof." [1] The New Compact Bible Dictionary goes well beyond that, and its entire definition and explanation of faith is worth sharing. It says, "Faith has both an active and passive sense; in the former, meaning 'fidelity,' 'trustworthiness;' in the latter, 'trust,' 'reliance.' An example of the first is found in Romans 3:3, where 'the faith of God' means His fidelity to promise. In the overwhelming majority of cases it has the meaning of reliance and trust.

"In the Old Testament (King James Version) the word 'faith' occurs only twice (Deuteronomy 32:20; Habakkuk 2:4), and even the verb form, 'to believe,' is far from common, appearing less than 30 times. What we find in the OT is not so much a doctrine of faith, as examples of it.

"In contrast with the extreme rarity with which the terms 'faith' and 'believe' are used in the OT, they occur with great frequency in the New Testament -- almost 500 times. A principal reason for this is that the NT makes the claim that the promised Messiah had finally come, and, to the bewilderment of many, the form of the fulfillment did not obviously correspond to the Messianic promise. It required a real act of faith to believe that Jesus of Nazareth was the promised Messiah. It was not long before 'to believe' meant to become a Christian. In the NT, faith therefore becomes supreme of all human acts and experiences.

"It is in Paul's epistles that the meaning of faith is most clearly and fully set forth. Faith is trust in the person of Jesus, the truth of His teaching, and the redemptive work He accomplished at Calvary. Faith is not to be confused with a mere intellectual assent to the doctrinal teachings of Christianity, though that is obviously necessary. It includes a radical and total commitment to Him as the Lord of one's life.

"Unbelief, or lack of faith in the Christian Gospel, appears everywhere in the NT as the supreme evil. Not to make a decisive response to God's offer in Christ means that the individual remains in his sin and is eternally lost. Faith alone can save him." [2]

From Where Does It Come?

Now that we know what it is, upon what is it developed? Where do we find it? From what is it extracted? The simplicity of the answers to those questions are accompanied by difficulties encountered in its establishment.

Faith is not developed upon anything previously existing. Intelligence and logic, based solely on what we can see, hear, smell, touch or taste, takes us to the edge of the cliff. Belief in a Supreme Being not experienced by our physical senses abides on the grassy knoll opposite the culmination of the Intelligence & Logic Trail. A deep and wide chasm separates the two. A leap is required. And there are no guarantees we will clear the ravine, nor like what we find if we do.

One of the greatest intellectual achievements of Western civilization is the Summa Theologica written by the medieval theologian Thomas Acquinas. It places anthropology, science, ethics, psychology, political theory and theology under God in an attempt to gather all truth into one coherent whole. This masterpiece contains thirty-eight treatises, three thousand articles and ten thousand objections.

Thomas abruptly stopped writing on December 6, 1273, however, when he caught a glimpse of eternity while officiating at a mass in the chapel of Saint Thomas. His secretary, Reginald, encouraged him to resume his writing. Holding fast to his decision to terminate his work, Thomas is said to have replied, "Reginald, I can do no more. Such things have been revealed to me that all I have written seems as so much straw." * Even the greatest of intellects fall far short of defining or explaining God.

Faith therefore cannot be earned, created, found, bought, borrowed or stolen -- it must be received. Paul said, "As God's messenger I give each of you God's warning: be honest in your estimate of yourselves, measuring your value by how much faith God has given you" (Romans 12:3). God simply gives it to us in the quantity He chooses us to have if we willingly receive it from Him. He forces nothing upon us. And this is where the leap is required since our insecure nature wants only what we can comprehend and control.

The Hebrews 11 passage recorded in the lesson summary persuades us to make this harrowing leap by explaining how eternally vital faith is. And although it's not extracted from anything, faith is motivated by something we all have in abundance. Our mortality and vulnerability to countless unavoidable calamities with all sorts of associated pain fills us with fear. It's obvious to even the most gifted and resourceful person on earth, that our capacity to control what comes upon us is incredibly limited. This is where faith comes in.

I read years ago about a wealthy engineer who was paranoid about fire in his home. He designed his elaborate house in a cautious manner, and had the most sophisticated fire prevention equipment installed. A few years later the electrical components of that system shorted out and his home burnt to the ground.

Fear Not

Our Creator knew that dread of the unknown and unknowable would haunt even the most courageous of men. Anxiety attempts to be the constant companion of each of us. The Lord, for that reason, admonishes us approximately three hundred and sixty-five times in His Word to "Fear Not."

It begins in the book of Genesis. God told Abraham to fear not since He was his shield and exceeding great reward (15:1). God told Abraham's concubine Hagar not to fear since He heard the cries of her son Ishmael (21:17). The Lord told Abraham's son Isaac not to fear since He is with him and will bless and multiply his descendents (26:24). And God likewise instructed Isaac's son Jacob not to fear going down to Egypt where he and his family would be saved from the famine and become a great nation there (46:3).

This process continues throughout the Old Testament. With the uncrossable Red Sea before them and the Egyptian Army on their unguarded flank, Moses instructed the Israelites not to fear. He said, "Do not be afraid. Stand firm and you will see the deliverance the Lord will bring you today. The Egyptians you see today you will never see again" (Exodus 14:13).

No one has had greater cause to fear than Joshua when he led the people of Israel into the land of Canaan. Seven nations, all of whom were greater than Israel, abided there within walled cities. Some were fierce giants. But the Lord said to him, "Have I not commanded you? Be strong and courageous. Do not be terrified; do not be discouraged, for the Lord your God will be with you wherever you go" (Joshua 1:9).

That book's historic account reveals God's faithfulness to those who trust in

Him. "Through three major military campaigns involving more than thirty enemy armies, the people of Israel learn a crucial lesson under Joshua's capable leadership: victory comes through faith in God and obedience to His Word, rather than through military might or numerical superiority." [3]

The "Fear Not" admonitions continue on. In the book of Judges, God told Gideon not to fear and that he would not die despite seeing the Angel of the Lord (6:32). He told the people of Israel, through Samuel, not to fear despite them turning away from Him. He promised not to forsake them as they return and serve Him (1 Samuel 12:20). Through the prophet Jahaziel, the Lord spoke to King Jehosaphat and all who lived in Judah and Jerusalem when a great multitude from Amon, Moab and Mount Seir gathered against them. He said, "Do not be afraid or discouraged because of this vast army. For the battle is not yours, but God's. . . You will not have to fight this battle. Take up your positions; stand firm and see the deliverance the Lord will give you, O Judah and Jerusalem. Do not be afraid; do not be discouraged. Go out to face them tomorrow, and the Lord will be with you" (2 Chronicles 20:15-17).

It happened just that way. When the people began to sing and praise the Lord, He caused the various nations in the enemy alliance to fight against one another until they were utterly destroyed. Judah won a great victory without lifting a hand against their enemies.

The fear nots are found in abundance throughout the remainder of the Old Testament. Search them out for yourself in your concordance. And they don't stop when you travel on into the New Testament. The angel told Mary not to fear because she had found favor with God (Luke 1:30). The angel told the shepherds not to fear as he brought them tidings of great joy (Luke 2:10). And Jesus told His apostles, "Do not be afraid of those who kill the body but cannot kill the soul.

Rather, be afraid of the one who can destroy both soul and body in hell" (Matthew 10:28).

You need to see in all of these passages the similar sequence despite very different circumstances. Fear, which is not seen but very real, paralyses those to whom God spoke. Only as they believed and did as they were told did the Lord act on their behalf. Then that which began in the spiritual world manifested itself in the physical realm. Hard and fast evidence proved time after time that God could be trusted to act on behalf of those who believed in Him. But faith in Him and His Word had to be their choice. It was given to them freely, but they had the liberty to reject it.

The Bible tells us that fear is a spirit, but is not of the Lord. He gives us power, love and a sound mind (2 Timothy 1:7). So our foundation of faith is simply a gift from God which is ours for the taking. Jesus said, "Do not let your hearts be troubled. Trust in God; trust also in me" (John 14:1).

Something to Trust In

I heard about a man who devised a simple but effective method for painting the window trim on his A-frame home. He tied a heavy-duty rope to the bumper of his car and threw it over the roof of the house. He walked up the other side of the roof by pulling on the rope, and tied it around his waist as he reached the windows.

A problem solver he was; a communicator he was not. Failing to tell his wife of his master plan, she got in the car and left for the store. He travelled swiftly up one side of the house and down the other, screaming to his spouse until he plowed the front yard. He somehow survived that bruising experience, and was far more cautious thereafter when choosing that in which he trusted.

Everyone seems to have faith in something or someone. The intellectuals in eighteenth century France believed that universal truth can be found only through human reason. This period, known as "The Enlightenment," led to perhaps mankind's most brutal and devastating revolution.

"The Enlightenment" ushered in what is known as "modernism" which has continued on despite its horrible consequences in France. This theory takes on many forms, but is based on the belief there is no God or single supreme authority, but each of us is capable of being a god, or is in fact a god.

The most pervasive intellectual doctrine of our day is called "postmodernism." It rejects all previous claims of man's ability to achieve any overarching, universal truth by teaching there is no such plan or purpose for our existence. These great thinkers proclaim there is no "grand metanarrative" -- nothing that makes sense of reality. They reject all claims of any form of worldview or master plan, but profess that life is a series of unconnected pieces which have no ultimate purpose or meaning. Postmodernism is essentially a belief in nothing coherent which then allegedly frees the individual to do as he chooses since there is no "cause and effect;" no consequences related to his/her actions. The result, of course, is total hopelessness which leads to depression, despondency and hostility. [4]

G. K. Chesterton once said, "The first effect of not believing in God is to believe in anything." In a similar manner, Chuck Colson says, "The opposite of Christianity isn't atheism; it's superstition and blind faith in any fad that happens along."

"Feng Shui" is a trendy new fad sweeping our post-Christian culture's spiritual gullibility. The term is Mandarin Chinese for "wind" and "water." It's a belief that buildings and landscapes are conduits for certain kinds of energy.

It may not totally surprise you that it's currently most prominent in Southern

California. The L.A. Times have reported that prospective homebuyers in their area actually have feng shui consultants to help them make the right choice. Some home-sale contracts even contain a feng shui contingency.

Savvy homeowners who understand the mindset of the modern buyer have their property pre-certified by a feng shui inspector. Of course this is only achieved after costly alterations are done to their home to assure that the "energy lines" flow unimpeded throughout the building's living space. There is no other way to receive a fair price in some sophisticated neighborhoods.

Unfortunately, this fanaticism hasn't been contained within California. A recent issue of Time magazine reported that feng shui enjoys a growing influence on corporate America. The article said that various real estate developers, Universal Studios, Merrill Lynch and Coty beauty products have all hired the same "consultant" to assist them in improving the energy flow within all their buildings. [5]

Our country became disconnected from the truth when it denounced Biblical Christianity. People are looking everywhere for answers and assurances, becoming vulnerable to anyone with persuasive abilities. Those who denounce scriptural absolutes validate P.T. Barnum's belief that "a sucker is born every minute."

I recently heard of a new and excellent book written by Dr. David Noebel called Understanding The Times (publisher unknown). It's a crash course in worldview analysis primarily for high school and college students. It teaches the reader to think biblically so they won't be confused nor misled in the classroom. He demonstrates how the three non-Christian worldviews influencing our society today -- Secular Humanism, Marxist-Leninism and Cosmic Humanism (new age spiritism) -- differ from Bible teachings.

Dr. Noebel divides worldview into ten categories: theology, philosophy, biology, ethics, psychology, sociology, law, politics, economics and history. He then teaches how these disciplines form a grid by which any worldview can be accurately analyzed alongside scriptural truth. It appears this book could be beneficial to many people beyond high school and college students. [6]

(Notes 4, 5 and 6 -- Copyright (c) 2000 Prison Fellowship Ministries. Reprinted with permission. "Breakpoint with Chuck Colson" is a radio ministry of Prison Fellowship.)

Chapter Eight Discovering Truth

Although faith is a gift that cannot be created, bought nor borrowed, it needs to be consistently developed. That only happens when our faith is regularly rewarded by the manifestation of what we believed in and hoped for. Knowledgeable and obedient students of God's Word are the only people on earth not frustrated and disappointed by that in which they trust.

Diligent Bible students have found over two hundred provable ways to develop their faith in God. These are known as His promises to heirs of His Covenant. Prior to looking at a few of them, it's essential to understand that each and every one has two parts. The first is called the "condition" which is what we must fully and accurately perform to put ourselves in position to receive God's "promise." That's the second part which the Lord can be relied upon to fulfill if the condition is met.

Most believers are acquainted with what are called Promise Books. They contain a full or partial listing of what God vows to do for those who do His will. All too often, however, the reader is simply encouraged to memorize and speak God's promise into their situation in order to receive its attainment. But that's not in accordance with biblical truth.

If you find such a book or list helpful, I encourage you to focus on the required condition. Know that God will not do our part and we can't do His. But as you will see shortly, He asks little of us compared to what He pledges in return.

A good parent attaches responsibility to privileges. When a father or mother promises a specific reward for certain tasks well done by their child, they should require diligent performance by the son or daughter before giving what was promised. But once the condition is met, it's essential they honor their word. Our Father in heaven has set that wise example.

Some Bible promises have a stated condition. The above analogy is an illustration of such. Many others, however, have an implied condition. This occurs when what is expected of us is so obvious that an explanation is unnecessary.

Consider the farmer as an analogy of implied faith. He works hard at plowing his field, fertilizing the soil, sowing seed and cultivating the plants. That's his part and as much as he can do. He realizes his dependence on forces beyond himself to cause the seed to germinate and provide adequate rain and sunshine essential to a healthy crop.

Without faith in God (or however he defines those forces), the farmer would lack motivation to perform his function well. But he can have no hope of an abundant harvest without doing his work in a responsible fashion. Farming is a joint venture with God, and so is the life of faith. Trusting in the Lord's integrity and ability to do as He promises is the foundation of growth in Christ.

Perform the Condition

In July, 1976, Israeli commandos made a daring raid at an airport in Entebbe, Uganda, in which 103 Jewish hostages were freed. In less than fifteen minutes, the soldiers had killed all seven of the kidnapers and set the captives free.

As successful as the rescue was, however, three of the hostages were killed during the raid. As the commandos entered the terminal, they shouted in Hebrew, "Get down! Crawl!" The Jewish hostages understood and laid down on the floor, while the guerrillas, who did not speak Hebrew, were left standing. The rescuers quickly shot the upright kidnapers.

But two of the hostages hesitated -- perhaps to see what was happening -- and were gunned down. One young man was lying down, but stood up when the commandos entered the airport and shouted their order. He, too, was killed by the bullets meant for the enemy. Had these three heeded the soldiers' command, they would have been freed with the rest of the captives. *

It's foolish not to do as instructed when you're depending on someone with credibility to perform for you that which you can't do for yourself. Refusing to take medicine according to the prescribed dosages and times prohibits your doctor's capacity to restore you to good health. And refusing or neglecting to do as the Bible instructs keeps the Lord from doing for us what He desires. Our heavenly Father won't destroy us by rewarding our disobedience.

Biblical Promises

Let's look at a small sample of biblical promises starting in the Old Testament. The Lord said to King Solomon one night, "If my people who are called by my name will humble themselves and pray and seek my face and turn from their wicked ways, then will I hear from heaven and will forgive their sin and will heal their land" (2 Chronicles 7:14). The psalmist said, "Who may ascend the hill of the Lord? Who may stand in his holy place? He who has clean hands and a pure heart, who does not lift up his soul to an idol or swear by what is false. He will receive blessing from the Lord and vindication from God his Savior" (Psalm 24:3-5). And Isaiah said, "but those who hope in the Lord will renew their strength. They will soar on wings like eagles; they will run and not grow weary, they will walk and not be faint" (Isaiah 40:31).

Turning now to the New Testament, Jesus said, "Therefore everyone who hears these words of mine and puts them into practice is like a wise man who built his house on the rock. The rain came down, the streams rose, and the winds blew and beat against that house; yet it did not fall because it had its foundation on the rock" (Matthew 7:24,25). The Lord also said, If you hold to my teaching, you are really my disciples. Then you will know the truth, and the truth will set you free" (John 8:31,32). And the Lord's brother James said, "But the man who looks intently into the perfect law that gives freedom, and continues to do this, not forgetting what he heard, but doing it -- he will be blessed in what he does" (James 1:25). (Emphasis added to above passages.)

Trust and Obey

Are most or all of the promised blessings that which can only be experienced in the eternal spiritual realm? Or does God really care about our earthly existence and real life needs, concerns, hopes; and is He willing to intervene and intercede in temporal matters on our behalf? If you believe the Lord literally means what He says throughout His Word, as I surely do, then you know that many of the promised blessings are to be enjoyed in this life.

An interesting article appeared in the Pittsburgh Post Gazette a little over a year ago. It read, "Traditionally, religion is viewed as a haven for the sick and afflicted; Jesus, when He walked the ancient Holy Land, often ministered first to the diseased. But what if the traditional view is wrong and belief actually promotes better health? To the exasperation of some academics, that is what a growing body of medical research is beginning to show.

"Recent studies indicate that men and women who practice in any of the mainstream faiths have above-average longevity, fewer strokes, less heart disease, less clinical depression, better immune-system function, lower blood pressure and fewer anxiety attacks, and they are much less likely to commit suicide than the population at large. These findings come from secular medical schools and schools of public health. . .

"In the most striking finding, Dr. Harold Koenig of Duke University Medical Center has calculated that, with regard to any mainstream faith, 'Lack of religious involvement has an effect on mortality that is equivalent to 40 years of smoking one pack of cigarettes per day.' . .

"Duke's Koenig says the association between religious participation and good health holds for almost all Christianity and Judaism. . .'The main distinction seems to be whether you are a regular practitioner,' Koenig says. 'Within Christianity there is very little difference in outcomes among the various denominations, except for nonmainstream denominations. Between Judaism and Christianity there is very little difference.' Positive results can pass between generations, too. When parents regularly attend worship services, they increase the odds that their children will live longer, healthier lives.

"For nonmainstream denominations, the story is different. Christian Scientists suffer some of the nation's worse longevity statistics, despite their denomination's claim to exalt health. The Faith Assembly, a Christian offshoot whose members may shun medical care, has horrible mortality figures. And when people join cults their health indicators fall off the bottom of the curve. . ." [7]

In reference to that article's first paragraph, the traditional view -- if by that is meant the scriptural text -- is not wrong. The Gospels make it clear that Jesus did primarily minister to the afflicted, distressed, oppressed and demon possessed;

because only those who needed help sought His blessings. And belief in Him did in fact promote better health in spirit soul and body. Those who realize they need help are still the only ones who come to the Lord; and belief in Him still provides it.

The late Presbyterian minister and Moody Bible Institute professor, John H. Sammis, said it this way in his hymn entitled "Trust and Obey":

"When we walk with the Lord in the light of His Word, what a glory He sheds on our way! While we do His good will He abides with us still, and with all who will trust and obey.

"Not a shadow can rise, not a cloud in the skies, but His smile quickly drives it away; not a doubt nor a fear, not a sigh nor a tear, can abide while we trust and obey.

"Not a burden we bear, not a sorrow we share, but our toil He doth richly repay;
not a grief nor a loss, not a frown nor a cross, but is blest if we trust and obey.

"But we never can prove the delights of His love until all on the altar we lay,
for the favor He shows and the joy He bestows are for them who will trust and obey.

"Then in fellowship sweet we will sit at His feet, or we'll walk by His side in the way; what He says we will do, where He sends we will go--Never fear, only trust and obey.

Chorus: "Trust and obey--for there's no other way to be happy in Jesus--but to trust and   obey."

Tough times, if not already here, are just around the corner. I feel certain of that. There will soon be unlimited potential for fears and concerns; many will be valid. Now is the time to develop an unflappable faith in our all-powerful God Who will shelter and be a shield to those who day after day, trust and obey.

Lesson Four
Add Goodness to Faith

A POPULAR SYNONYM OF GOODNESS is virtue, and various Bible translations use it in place of goodness in 2 Peter 1:5. It's defined as right thinking and action. An ancient Persian proverb says, "Sow a thought, reap an act. Sow an act, reap a habit. Sow a habit, reap your character. Sow your character, reap your destiny." Virtuous thinking and doing is therefore the essential first step in directing your life down God's chosen path.

Chapter Nine Sow   Reap Principle

A young fighter pilot assigned to a carrier in the Pacific, Butch O'Hare, was one of many heroes produced by World War II. On a particular mission, he realized his fuel tank had not been topped off; thus he would not have sufficient fuel to complete his task and return to the ship. His flight leader ordered him back to the carrier.

He reluctantly dropped out of formation. But on his way back, he spotted a squadron of Japanese Zeroes headed towards the all but defenseless American fleet. There was no time to chase after his squadron to bring them back, nor was he able to warn the ships of the approaching danger.

His only hope was to divert the Japanese planes from their mission. With a total disregard for his own safety, he charged the group of Zeroes, attacking one after another. With reckless abandon, he broke their formation, expended his ammunition and used desperation maneuvers to inflict as much damage as possible upon the enemy craft. The exasperated Japanese squadron finally took off in another direction.

Butch O'Hare and his tattered fighter limped back to the carrier. He related his tale to the naval commanders, supporting it with the film from the camera mounted on the plane. He was awarded one of the nation's highest military honors, and Chicago's international airport is named after him in tribute to the unselfish courage of its distinguished flying son.

Let's remain in the "Windy City" and pick up on the life of one it is not so proud of. During the prohibition and depression years, a man called Easy Eddie served as counselor for the notorious Al Capone. He was a gifted attorney who used his legal maneuvering skill to keep the gangster and his mob out of prison.

Easy Eddie was well compensated, and he and his family lived in a mansion on an estate which occupied an entire city block. Despite his disregard for the atrocity wrought by those he enthusiastically defended, he had a soft spot for his young son. In addition to giving him the best of everything, he worked at teaching him right from wrong. He wanted his son to rise above the sordid life in which he, himself, was ensnared; and become a man of value to society.

This major internal conflict eventually took its toll, and Eddie finally accepted what he always knew. His grand expectation for his son was only possible if he became a better example for him to follow. The hypocrisy in which he lived would negate all of his efforts and high hopes.

He made a most difficult decision, and submitted himself to the authorities as a witness who would testify against Scarface Al Capone and his mob. He knew the great risk he was taking, but was willing to do so for the sake of his son. And within the year, he was gunned down on a lonely Chicago street.

Nothing in that great city is named after Easy Eddie, even though its international airport bears his surname. That's because World War II hero Lieutenant Commander Edward "Butch" O'Hare was the son he died for.

Many lessons can be learned from these documented true stories, but perhaps the most important is that which Paul taught in Galatians 6:7. This passage says, "Do not be deceived; God cannot be mocked. A man reaps what he sows." The longer we ignore God's admonition to do things His way, the greater will be the difficulty encountered and the price paid. It's good from an eternal standpoint Easy Eddie attempted to right his wrongs, but the hole he dug was so deep he was buried in it.

There are two separate but integrated types of character traits. The first set forms your foundation by defining what you are. The second is governed by the first and determines what you do. The quality of the foundational traits influence the standard of one's performance in the various aspects of life. So we will begin with the building blocks of integrity.

What You Are

Honesty is the refusal to steal, cheat or lie; being upright and trustworthy. It is an all or nothing characterization. Be honest most of the time but compromise periodically for a selfish pursuit, and you will be perceived as a dishonest person. On the other hand, strive to be honest in the hidden and little things as well as the big matters, and you will achieve the respect of many. As the Reverend Dwight L. Moody said, "Character is what you are in the dark."

In a particular Peanuts comic strip created by Charles Schultz, it was the first day of the new school year, and the students were told to write an essay about returning to class. Lucy wrote, "Vacations are nice, but it's good to get back to school. There is nothing more satisfying or challenging than education, and I look forward to a year of expanding my knowledge."

The teacher expressed her delight with that essay, and Lucy leaned over and whispered to Charlie Brown, "After a while, you learn what sells." *

Honesty doesn't always achieve what you want in the short term, but it's the only path on which you continue moving forward without regrets and the need to alter your course. Proverbs 11:3 says, "The integrity of the upright guides them, but the unfaithful are destroyed by their duplicity." And 12:22 says, "The Lord detests lying lips, but he delights in men who are truthful."

Humility is the acknowledgment of one's own weaknesses and faults, as well as the honest appraisal of one's strengths, talents and abilities. It's falsely understood as being self-abasement, an unwillingness to assert oneself in any way, and the taking of a backseat to others at all times.

A humble person, in many cases, stands out in a group and is often seen as a competent leader. That's because he accepts himself for what he is, learns how to keep his frail and weak areas from hurting himself and others, and diligently develops the gifts God gave him. He likewise appreciates the talents and abilities he sees in others; recognizes how fragile life is on this cold, hard and impersonal planet; and readily admits his need for God and others to live this life in a meaningful and successful manner. As proverbs 22:4 says, "Humility and the fear of the Lord bring wealth and honor and life."

It is said the freed slave, George Washington Carver, prayed: "O Great God, show me the secrets of Your universe." The Lord allegedly replied, "O little man, you could not begin to comprehend such things. I will instead show you the secrets of the peanut." Carver then spent the remainder of his life wearing tattered clothes, living in austerity and discovering hundreds of uses of this simple dry fruit and other things for the benefit of the common man. Despite rejecting the relative degree of fame and fortune offered him, even the white science community came to recognize his God-given genius.

Contentment is being happy with what one has or is; not wanting anything else; a feeling of quiet satisfaction. Hebrews 13:5 says, "Keep your lives free from the love of money and be content with what you have, because God has said,

'Never will I leave you; never will I forsake you.'"

The evidence of contentment is good stewardship. A contented person thanks God daily for what he has, and diligently cares for and maintains all of it. He begins each day with time with his Creator, seeing it as a privilege to do so. He appreciates and nurtures the spouse God gave him, and attends to the needs of his children. He is thankful for a healthy body and regularly exercises, keeps to a healthy diet and gets sufficient rest. He is likewise happy with his material blessings, keeps them secure and in good condition, and uses them wisely.

A school teacher lost her life savings in a business scheme that had been elaborately explained by a swindler. She went to the Better Business Bureau after her investment disappeared and her dream was shattered.

An official there asked why she didn't come to them first to check out the legitimacy of that particular involvement. The woman reluctantly, but honestly , admitted that she didn't go to the Better Business Bureau first because she was afraid they would tell her not to do it. * Those who are not contented with what they have often lose it all and live to regret it.

Faithfulness means to be deserving of trust; being loyal and dependable. Proverbs 11:6 says, "The righteousness of the upright delivers them, but the unfaithful are trapped by evil desires." Verse 20:6 says, "Many a man claims to have unfailing love, but a faithful man who can find?" And 28:20 says, "A faithful man will be richly blessed, but one eager to get rich will not go unpunished."

I've read about the birth process of giraffes. The female of the specie delivers her calf while standing, permitting it to fall approximately ten feet and land on its back. The baby giraffe rolls to an upright position with its legs tucked under its body, then shakes off the birthing fluid from its eyes and ears.

At that point, mom takes a quick look at her offspring, then positions herself directly over it. She then swings a long, pendulous leg outward and kicks her baby, sending it sprawling. She repeats this process until the calf finally forces itself to stand for the first time on wobbly legs. Then to help it remember how it got up, she kicks it again, knocking it off its feet.

Female giraffes intuitively know that in the wilds of Africa their young are most vulnerable. Safety is found within the herd, and the calves must be able to arise quickly and run with it when danger approaches. Lions, hyenas, leopards and wild hunting dogs enjoy young giraffes, and they get them when mom doesn't apply this harsh method to teach it how to protect itself. *

The faithful parent, spouse or friend always does or says what's best for the other person. It is quite often not what's easy or popular, but that is not their concern. How can I help my child? What does my spouse need that I can provide? What would be in the best interest of my friend? How can I be there for those who need me? These are the only questions asked or issues considered by a faithful person.

Self-denial is the act of giving up or refraining for a time from what one wants for the long-term betterment of self, and thus benefit to others. This is the linchpin character trait. The refusal to exercise self-discipline and deny our carnal appetites compromises the other qualities. Conversely, those other traits are strengthened when we look to God daily for the help to deny ourselves of what is harmful to us and our loved ones.

We are spirit, soul and body. An absence of self-denial in one separate but integrated aspect of our being, adversely affects the other two.

Paul said, "Everything is permissible for me -- but not everything is beneficial. Everything is permissible for me -- but I will not be mastered by anything" (1 Corinthians 6:12). And Solomon said, "The evil deeds of a wicked man ensnare him; the cords of his sin hold him fast. He will die for lack of discipline, led astray by his own great folly" (Proverbs 5:22,23).

What You Do

Ben Franklin is label by many historians as an agnostic, yet had a thirty year close friendship with Britain's and America's great evangelist, George Whitefield. Having an obvious affinity for religion, Franklin spent years seeking progressive personal perfection by developing the virtues of temperance, silence, order, resolution, frugality, industry, sincerity, justice, moderation, cleanliness, tranquility and chastity. Unfortunately, he grew careless in his later years and permitted his standards of behavior to deteriorate somewhat. The cause of his inability to endure to the end is reflected in one of his late-in-life writings wherein he stated, "Mr. Whitefield used to pray for my conversion but never had the satisfaction of feeling that his prayers were heard." [1]

Many folks try hard to change themselves by their own efforts. Those with destructive habits such as alcoholism and drug addiction seek help from groups dedicated to treating those "diseases." Some experience a reasonable degree of success, but they limit themselves to their own ability and determination to keep the cause of the problem, man's depraved nature, in hibernation.

Spiritual rebirth, achieved by repenting and accepting Christ as Lord and Savior, provides the only opportunity for total victory over our innate weak and sinful ways. Paul said, "You were taught, with regard to your former way of life, to put off your old self, which is being corrupted by its deceitful desires; to be made new in the attitude of your minds; and to put on the new self, created to be like God in true righteousness and holiness" (Ephesians 4:22-24).

Now that we know what must first occur to become ever more Christ-like, let's look at Ben Franklin's desirable dozen:

Temperance is the taking care to keep one's actions, appetites, feelings, etc. under proper control. Paul said, "And everyone who competes for the prize is temperate in all things. Now they do it to obtain a perishable crown, but we for an imperishable crown" (1 Corinthians 9:25) (NKJV). We won't win our race without discipline and self-control which is temperance.

Silence is being still and not speaking. Solomon said, "There is a time for everything, and a season for every activity under heaven. . . a time to be silent and a time to speak" (Ecclesiastes 3:1&7). He also said, "When words are many, sin is not absent, but he who holds his tongue is wise" (Proverbs 10:19). The Lord's brother James said, "My dear brothers, take note of this: Everyone should be quick to listen, slow to speak and slow to become angry" (James 1:19). Silence is essential for hearing the still small voice of the Holy Spirit.

Order means having everything in their proper place and functioning well. Speaking of church services, Paul said, "everything should be done in a fitting and orderly way" (1 Corinthians 14:40). All aspects of our daily life should be maintained accordingly.

Resolution means to be determined and decisive. Joshua resolved at an early age to serve the Lord, and never wavered from that commitment. Late in his life, after encouraging the nation of Israel to fear and obey God, he challenged them to make their own resolution. He said, "But if serving the Lord seems undesirable to you, then choose for yourselves this day whom you will serve. . . But as for me and my household, we will serve the Lord" (Joshua 24:15). In other words, "Don't be a hypocrite – be honest. Decide to live your life God's way or man's way; stick to it and accept the consequences of your choice."

Economy is being prudent in all of your expenditures; the preservation of time, energy, money and all other resources. Proverbs say, "The wisdom of the prudent is to give thought to their ways, but the folly of fools is deception." "The simple inherit folly, but the prudent are crowned with knowledge." And "through knowledge its (house built by wisdom) rooms are filled with rare and beautiful treasures" (Proverbs 14:8 & 18; 24:4).

Industry is the practice of working hard and steady with diligence. The first king of the northern portion of the divided nation of Israel was an excellent worker. "The man Jeroboam was a mighty man of valor; and Solomon, seeing that the young man was industrious, made him the officer over all the labor force of the house of Joseph" (1 Kings 11:28) (NKJV). Although he subsequently chose to depart from the ways of God which ultimately destroyed him, his industry provided the opportunity to be used in a significant and meaningful position.

Sincerity means to be without pretense, deception or false implications. Uncompromised sincerity in all matters will enable us to say as did Paul, "We are so glad that we can say with utter honesty that in all our dealings we have been pure and sincere, quietly depending upon the Lord for his help, and not on our own skills" (2 Corinthians 1:12) (TLB).

Justice means to provide or cause to occur that which is right, fair, honest and proper. The psalmist contemplated the goodness and integrity of the Lord and proclaimed, "Righteousness and justice are the foundation of your throne; love and faithfulness go before you" (Psalm 89:14). One of the purposes for the writing of Proverbs was "for acquiring a disciplined and prudent life, doing what is right and just and fair;" because "To do what is right and just is more acceptable to the Lord than sacrifice" (Proverbs 1:3 & 21:3). Justice should preside within the home, church, workplace, governmental council and judicial proceeding; and each of us is responsible for bringing it into our corner of the world.

Moderation is the avoiding of harmful extremes in thought, attitude, action and response. Maintaining a balanced approach in all areas keeps us in the middle of the path of life. The Bible (King James Version) uses the term just once, but explicitly encourages us to live in a reasonable and proper manner. Much of Proverbs and the Gospel teachings of Jesus instructs us to employ wisdom and good judgment in all matters, and that is moderation.

Cleanliness is being clean, neat and orderly in thought, speech, habits and personal appearance. Moral pollution abounds in modern day America. And the hectic pace required by our materialistic mindset causes many to be sloppy within their affairs, assignments and abode. David cried out to the Lord, "Create in me a clean heart, O God, and renew a steadfast spirit within me" (Psalm 51:10). His son Solomon asked the question, "Who can say, 'I have kept my heart pure; I am clean without sin'?" (Proverbs 20:9). None can make that claim, but a daily effort should be made to achieve cleanliness of spirit, soul and body.

Tranquility results from a calm, quiet and peaceful temperament and demeanor. Daniel spoke to King Nebuchadnezzar relative to interpreting his disturbing dream, saying "Therefore, O king, let my counsel be acceptable to you; break off your sins by practicing righteousness, and your iniquities by showing mercy to the oppressed, that there may perhaps be a lengthening of your tranquility" (Daniel 4:27) (RSV).

Chastity is pure and moral behavior. Little need be said here as much effort is required to resist the unrelenting temptation imposed upon us by our decadent society.

Paul demonstrated the intense integration of the "what we are" and the "what we do" traits in his letter to Titus. He said, "You must teach what is in accord with sound doctrine. Teach the older men to be temperate, worthy of respect, self-controlled, and sound in faith, in love and in endurance. Likewise, teach the older women to be reverent in the way they live, not to be slanderers or addicted to much wine, but to teach what is good. Then they can train the younger women to love their husbands and children, to be self-controlled and pure, to be busy at home, to be kind, and to be subject to their husbands, so that no one will malign the Word of God. Similarly, encourage the young men to be self-controlled. In everything set them an example by doing what is good. In your teaching show integrity, seriousness and soundness of speech that cannot be condemned, so that those who oppose you may be ashamed because they have nothing bad to say about us" (Titus 2:1-8).

Three Essentials for Christian Leadership

The following character traits are complimentary to and an extension of those listed above. They were provided by Ted Engstrom in his Motivation To Last A Lifetime:

Enthusiasm is optimism and hope, seeing opportunity in every difficulty; the ability to laugh about unpleasant situations in order to forget them.

Trustworthiness is being honest and transparent in all dealings and relationships; having deep integrity without compromise in both small and the more significant issues.

Christian Discipline is the condition of being conquered by Christ's love; being never too busy to care and always available to reach out to someone in need. It's studying while others waste time; praying while others play; modeling the behavior of the Master.

Personal Confidence is believing in oneself so others can also.

Decisiveness means the ability to make a swift and clear decision once all the facts are in; resisting the temptation to procrastinate in drawing an intelligent conclusion; refusing to vacillate once the decision is made.

Courage is the ability to stay in there five minutes longer; being scared without capitulating to the fear.

Sense of Humor enables the leader to relax tensions and relieve difficult situations with clean, wholesome humor. It's the ability to laugh at oneself, and create a pleasant and enjoyable environment where people can laugh together and work in unity and harmony.

Loyalty is the most important leadership trait, and is expressed in commitment, steadfastness and faithfulness to those served. [2]

Chapter Ten When Goodness is Lacking

During the year 2000, the internet provided the following astounding statistics relative to just one organization with a little over five hundred members:

29 have been accused of spousal abuse.

7 have been arrested for fraud.

19 have been accused of writing bad checks.

117 have bankrupted at least two businesses.

3 have been arrested for assault.

71 can't get a credit card due to bad credit.

14 have been arrested on drug related charges.

8 have been arrested for shoplifting.

21 are current defendants in law suits.

84 were stopped for drunk driving during 1998.

Assuming those statistics are accurate, does it shock you that the above acts were committed by the 535 members of the then existing United States Congress? Considering that these are the men and women charged with the responsibility of writing the laws of this land, would you say that virtuous leaders are essential for good government, sound schools and churches, honest enterprises and solid families? Since goodness is obviously lacking in high places in this country, might tough times be just ahead?

Wisdom Required

The Open Bible Expanded Edition's prelude to the Book of Proverbs says, "The key word in Proverbs is wisdom, 'the ability to live life skillfully.' A godly life in an ungodly world, however, is no simple assignment. Proverbs provides God's detailed instructions for His people to deal successfully with the practical affairs of everyday life: how to relate to God, parents, children, neighbors, and government. Solomon, the principal author, uses a combination of poetry, parables, pithy questions, short stories, and wise maxims to give in strikingly memorable form the common sense and divine perspective necessary to handle life's issues." [3]

A large, ethical company wanted their employees to be capable of making a clear distinction between a wise person and a fool. They circulated the following to achieve that purpose:

A wise person says, "Let's find out;" a fool says, "Nobody knows."

When a mistake is made, a wise person says, "I was wrong;" but a fool says, "It wasn't my fault."

A wise person isn't nearly as afraid of losing as a fool is secretly afraid of winning.

The wise person works harder than a fool and has more time; a fool is always "too busy" to do what is necessary.

A wise person goes through a problem; a fool goes around it, and never gets past it.

A wise person makes commitments; a fool makes promises.

A wise person says, "I'm good, but not as good as I could or should be." A fool says,   "I'm not as bad as a lot of other people."

A wise person listens; a fool just waits until it's his/her turn to talk.

A wise person respects those who are superior and tries to learn something from them.   A fool resents those who are superior and looks for chinks in their armor.

A wise person explains; a fool explains away.

A wise person feels responsible for more than his/her job. A fool says, "I only work   here."

A wise person says, "There ought to be a better way to do it." A fool says, "That's the

way it has always been done."

A wise person paces himself; a fool has just two speeds--hysterical and lethargic.

We obviously have a free-will and many choices to make each day. They then determine if we are wise or foolish, victorious or defeated. Goodness is the prerequisite for godly wisdom, and is difficult to achieve since it mandates the overcoming of our innate self-centered nature. But Jesus said, "To him who overcomes, I will give the right to sit with me on my throne, just as I overcame and sat down with my Father on his throne" (Revelation 3:21).

What Throne?

The throne the Lord speaks of is that which He will occupy during His one thousand year "Millennium" reign on earth, which is the final event preceding eternity with God in heaven. The "Rapture," the initial end-time event, is the culmination of the New Testament Church that began on Pentecost, and will occur prior to the "Tribulation." The Rapture is separate and distinct from the "Second Coming" of Christ to earth which is the Lord's promised return for the faithful remnant of His nation Israel, and all others who submit to Him during the seven year Tribulation period. All who received Salvation during the "Church Age" (Pentecost to the Rapture) return and rule with the Lord during the Millennium reign.

The Bible states that the Rapture is the start of end-time happenings, and is imminent. Dr. Renald Showers, a renown expert on the Rapture of the Church, defines the term imminent as follows: "An imminent event is one which is always 'hanging overhead, is constantly ready to befall or overtake one; close at hand in its incidence' ('imminent,' The Oxford English Dictionary, 1901, V, 66.). Thus, imminence carries the sense that it could happen at any moment. Other things may happen before the imminent event, but nothing else must take place before it happens. If something else must take place before an event can happen, then that event is not imminent. In other words, the necessity of something else taking place first destroys the concept of imminency.

"Since a person never knows exactly when an imminent event will take place, then he cannot count on a certain amount of time transpiring before the imminent event happens. In light of this, he should always be prepared for it to happen at any moment. . .

"The imminent coming of Christ should have an incredible practical effect on the lives of individual Christians and the church as a whole. The fact that the glorified, holy Son of God could step through the door of heaven at any moment is intended by God to be the most pressing, incessant motivation for holy living and aggressive ministry (including missions, evangelism, and Bible teaching), and the greatest cure for lethargy and apathy. It should make a major difference in every Christian's values, actions, priorities and goals." [4]

Dr. Showers agrees with the apostle Peter who said it this way: "And so since everything around us is going to melt away, what holy, godly lives we should be living! You should look forward to that day and hurry it along -- the day when God will set the heavens on fire, and the heavenly bodies will melt and disappear in flames. But we are looking forward to God's promise of new heavens and a new earth afterwards, where there will be only goodness" (2 Peter 3:11-13). (TLB) (Emphasis added)

LESSON FIVE
ADD KNOWLEDGE TO GOODNESS

SINCE IT'S TIME TO ADD KNOWLEDGE to goodness, here's a relevant story. A shepherd was tending to his large flock in a field by a deserted country road when a black Jeep Grand Cherokee with gold trim drove up and stopped. The driver, a young man dressed in a Brioni suit, Cerutti shoes, Ray-Ban glasses, Jovial Swiss watch and Bhs tie, emerged and approached the shepherd. "If I guess how many sheep you have, will you give me one of them?," asked the stylish gentleman.

The shepherd, somewhat amused but mostly curious, agreed to do so. The young man returned to his sports utility vehicle, connected his notebook and mobile fax, entered a NASA web site, scanned the ground using his GPS, opened a database and 60 excel tables filled with logarithms, then printed a 150 page report on his high-tech mini-printer.

He went back to the shepherd and said, "You have exactly 1,677 sheep here." The shepherd concurred and honored his promise to give up one of them. The young man selected his animal and loaded it in the Jeep.

Just before driving away, the shepherd asked if he could have his animal back if he guessed the young man's occupation. The pompous fellow assumed this hick was incapable of knowing his modern big-city line of work, so he agreed. The shepherd then stated, "You are a consultant!"

Astounded, the young man asked how he could know that. The wise, old shepherd replied, "You came without being called; charged a fee for telling me something I already knew; and it's obvious you know nothing about my business since you took my dog."

People who pretend to have all the answers and know your business better than you have always been around. The computer age, however, has caused them to proliferate. They abound with charts, graphs, analyses and 150 page reports.

Their plethora of information, fact or otherwise, disguises itself as knowledge essential for your best interest. Using you to obtain what they want, however, is their real objective.

An ancient proverb says, "He who knows not but knows not that he knows not, is a fool -- avoid him. He who knows not but knows that he knows not, is a child -- teach him. He who knows but knows not that he knows, is asleep -- awaken him. And he who knows and knows that he knows, is a sage -- follow him." Ask God for the wisdom to discern into which of the above categories those whom you encounter belong.

Information and practical knowledge are related, but not as identical twins. Information is comprised of findings, news, statistics, results, etc. Practical knowledge is information beneficial to its user for a specific purpose. The same information may be beneficial to one person while useless or harmful to another.

A sign on a pickup truck said, "Elucidate! Don't obfuscate!" In other words, "Explain in a simple and clear manner. Don't confuse the issue or fog up the truth with impertinent or misleading information." To be practical, knowledge must be offered or made available in a comprehensible manner. To be applicable, information must be compatible with one's values, desires, priorities and circumstances. The glut of information spewing from the electronic media these days often fails to meet that criteria.

Those who followed the murder trial involving a prominent sports personality a few years ago saw obfuscation elevated to a science. The high-profile team of defense attorneys, for the sole purpose of diverting attention and fogging-up what appeared to be indisputable evidence of the defendant's guilt, inundated the jury with issues involving the investigation and other extraneous matters. He walked away a free man.

The regularly exercised, well conditioned mind is not readily deceived, diverted or disconcerted. It discerns the facts, discards the fiction and disregards the irrelevant.

Chapter Eleven The Essence of Practical Knowledge

Some passages require repeating. Hosea 4:6 says, "My people are destroyed for lack of knowledge. Because you have rejected knowledge, I also reject you as My priest; because you have ignored the law of your God, I also will ignore your children."

Hosea spoke of the knowledge God gave to Moses for governing His chosen people. An updated interpretation would include all of the instructions for righteous living given by the Holy Spirit to the forty writers of the Old and New Testaments. People who reject the Bible as the inerrant word of God continue to be destroyed and take their children with them. The Hosea passage still warns God's creation of the danger of ignoring or disobeying the Creator's guidance.

Another part of the Old Testament provides further insight into the importance God places on wisdom and knowledge of His ways. He appeared to Solomon the night he and all the congregation had gone up to Gibean, the place where the tabernacle of meeting with God rested. The Lord said to him, "Ask for whatever you want me to give you." After thanking Him for His great mercies to his father David and causing him (Solomon) to succeed his father, Solomon responded to the

Lord's request.

"Give me wisdom and knowledge that I may lead this people , for who is able to govern this great people of yours?" God replied, "Since this is your heart's desire and you have not asked for wealth, riches or honor, nor for the death of your enemies, and since you have not asked for a long life but for wisdom and knowledge to govern my people over whom I have made you king, therefore wisdom and knowledge will be given you. And I will also give you wealth, riches and honor, such as no king who was before you ever had and after you will have" (2 Chronicles 1:3-12).

Centuries later, Paul had this to say to his disciple Timothy: "The whole Bible was given to us by inspiration from God and is useful to teach us what is true and to make us realize what is wrong in our lives; it straightens us out and helps us do what is right. It is God's way of making us well prepared at every point, fully equipped to do good to everyone (2 Timothy 3:16,17) (TLB).

Practical knowledge is restricted to that which helps us maximize our potential and impact our corner of the world. It's comprised of all that permeates our thoughts, words and deeds in accordance with God's plan for our lives.

Knowledge that controls, demeans or teaches the way to defraud and take advantage of others is well beyond those boundaries. Knowledge that puffs up and promotes arrogance, and knowledge for the sake of knowledge, are likewise not included here. Much of what our society lauds as brilliance is useless or even harmful. Most radical and destructive causes throughout history have been initiated and advanced by academics. And countless others among the most learned have lived unproductive lives due to their inability to accept reality and relate to others.

Does God's Way Really Work?

One evening during 1997, a radio commentator spoke of a recent study conducted to determine the cause of the substantial decline in the strength and stability of the Mafia within the United States. It was hoped that the findings would conclude that law enforcement agencies have discovered the inherent weaknesses in that crime alliance; and that those weaknesses and the most effective means of exploiting them could be clearly defined and cataloged.

The results of the study were startling. The extensive deterioration of the American family unit, and not our crime-stoppers, get much of the credit. When the family was strong and stable, resting upon the virtues of trust, faithfulness, loyalty, honesty, communication and authentic concern for one another, the Mafia was likewise strong and stable. "Crime families" evolved from relational units in Europe that united to protect one another during perilous times. And even though their mission and methods became evil and detrimental to humanity, they prospered while they emulated a healthy family. But as our culture's values eroded and undermined the foundation of society's most basic and vital component, the same occurred within the family structure of the Mafia. And thus it is crumbling. [1]

The researchers were stunned, but Bible students acquainted with that study are not at all surprised. The Kingdom Principal of Unity and Harmony essentially says, "Together we rise; divided we fall." Or as Jesus said, "Every kingdom divided against itself will be ruined, and every city or household divided against itself will not stand" (Matthew 12:25). And like all immutable God-ordained spiritual laws, the desired result is achieved when obeyed. It doesn't matter who does it so long as they do it God's way.

A 3/14/04 Pittsburgh Tribune-Review article told about the importing of

Sicilian gangsters to fill gaps in struggling American Mafiosi caused by new racketeering laws and a large increase in turncoats. Sicilians are thought to be far more inclined to keep the sacred vow of silence, thus remaining loyal to the crime family no matter the circumstances.

The American La Cosa Nostra are also sending their members to the island for lessons in thuggery. Sicilian mobster Antonio Giuffre said, "They send them here to make them become men of honor, to make them do training, because in America there's this attack on the values – there' no respect anymore. The American Mafia is different and it needs some of our qualities."

Further Evidence

A fascinating experience reported by World War II correspondent Clarence W. Hall occurred in early 1945. As U.S. forces pushed deep into Okinawa, they came across a village unlike any they had seen. Its name was Shimabuku, and the advancing troops were met by two old men and invited in as fellow Christians.

The reporter described the hamlet like this: "We'd seen other Okinawan villages, uniformly down at the heels and despairing; by contrast, this one shone like a diamond in a dung heap. Everywhere we went we were greeted by smiles and dignified bows. Proudly the old men showed us their spotless homes, their terraced fields, fertile and neat, their storehouses and granaries, and their prized sugar mill."

Hall uncovered an incredible story from his search for an answer as to why this village shined so brightly amidst such darkness. Some 30 years earlier, an American missionary on his way to Japan had stopped at Shimabuku, and stayed just long enough to make two converts and leave them a Japanese Bible. These new believers, with instructions just to read the Bible and live by it, began sharing their faith with neighbors. Before long the whole town had accepted Christ, and for 30 years had been diligently obeying God's Word.

They adopted the Ten Commandments as their legal code, and the Sermon on the Mount as their guide in social conduct. They taught the Bible in their schools, and their courts made decisions based on instructions found in God's Word.

Hall noted that they managed to create a Christian democracy in its purest sense. The result was that there were no jails, no saloons, no drunkenness, no divorce, and a high level of happiness.

The young war correspondent requisitioned a jeep and investigated the town more thoroughly. He attended a primitive but deeply spiritual worship service and came away impressed. Upon leaving Shimabuku, his jeep driver said, "So this is what comes out of just a Bible and two old guys who wanted to live like Jesus. Maybe we're using the wrong weapons to make this world over." [2]

God's way obviously works, and very well at that. But the people of God must first submit to Jesus as Lord, then to His Word as law. They must study the Scriptures, understand them and practically apply them to all aspects of their lives. The Senate Chaplain, Pastor LLoyd John Ogilvie, said, "The greatest single cause of impaired hearing of fresh truth is the refusal to live what we know already." [3]

Chapter Twelve What We Must Know To Be Saved

Much knowledge is required to live our earthly existence successfully in a purposeful manner. But we won't have the peace and serenity essential for the abundant life Jesus offers until we are assured we will spend eternity with Him.

With that in mind, let's inquire of Jesus as did the lawyer in Luke 10:25 and the ruler in Luke 18:18. The question asked by each was, "Teacher, what must I do to inherit eternal life?"

Jesus answered the lawyer with a question of His own, saying, "What is written in the Law? How do you read it?" The lawyer's answer was, "Love the Lord your God with all your heart and with all your soul and with all your strength and with all your mind; and, love your neighbor as yourself" (Luke 10:26,27).

As the Lord explained to His disciples, "If you love me, you will obey what I command" (John 14:15). And, "Whoever has my commands and obeys them, he is the one who loves me" (John 14:21).

In response to the ruler, Jesus said, "You know the commandments: Do not commit adultery, do not murder, do not steal, do not give false testimony, honor your father and mother" (Luke 18:20).

Those passages state that obeying the Ten Commandments is essential to being saved. Since we can't obey what we don't know, it's important to study the details of those directives which are found in Exodus 20 and Deuteronomy 5. Obeying the first four demonstrates our love for God, and observing the last six testifies of our love for others.

The full Salvation message, meaning the biblical order for saving one's soul, is "repent and believe." Jesus stressed this by repeating to His disciples in Luke 13:5, "but unless you repent you will all likewise perish." Unfortunately, just the second part is taught in many contemporary churches. Yet it's obvious that the "hearing of faith" or the "love, mercy and grace of God only" message has produced many decisions for Christ, but no true Salvation.

The truth is that regardless of one's belief in Jesus, he can't be saved without repentance. And he can't repent unless he knows what sin is. Thus he remains in his sin until he acquires knowledge of the Ten Commandments, then asks the Lord's forgiveness for his prior transgressions.

A lawless gospel produces lawless converts – those who name the name of Christ but never depart from disobedience. These are the ones who approach Jesus at the final judgment and say, "Lord, Lord, did we not prophesy in your name, and in your name drive out demons and perform many miracles?" And they are the ones to whom Jesus will speak those dreaded words, "I never knew you. Away from me, you evildoers!" (Matthew 7:22,23).

The famed Bible commentator, Matthew Henry, said, "There is no way of coming to that knowledge of sin which is necessary to repentance, and consequently to peace and pardon, but by comparing our hearts and lives with the Law." [4]

The great nineteenth century American evangelist, Charles Finney, taught that "Evermore the Law must prepare the way for the Gospel. To overlook this in instructing souls, is almost certain to result in false hope, the introduction of a false standard of Christian experience, and to fill the Church with false converts." (4)

The brilliant nineteenth century London pastor Charles Haddon Spurgeon said, "Lower the Law and you dim the light by which man perceives his guilt; this is a very serious loss to the sinner rather than a gain; for it lessens the likelihood of his conviction and conversion. . . Therefore the Law serves a most necessary and blessed purpose, and it must not be removed from its place." (4)

The author of Pilgrim's Progress, John Bunyan, said, "The man who does not know the nature of the Law, cannot know the nature of sin." (4) And Jesus validates what's written above when He says, "Not everyone who says to me, 'Lord, Lord,' will enter the kingdom of heaven, but only he who does the will of my Father who is in heaven" (Matthew 7:21).

Knowing and Doing God's Will

The gifted writer and teacher, Phillip Keller, devotes an entire chapter to the phrase "Thy will be done" in his A Layman Looks At The Lord's Prayer. The following co-mingled excerpts from that chapter provide assistance in defining how to know, and then do, God's will for your life.

Phillip Keller said, "It is traditionally true to say that uncounted millions of men and women have repeated these four words (Thy will be done) without having the faintest idea what God's will is. It is even more sobering to reflect that even more people have repeated them without any intention whatever of seeing to it that our Father's will is done; even if they did know it. So in a sense there is much vain and pointless repetition of a phrase which actually bears enormous import for the Christian."

Prior to teaching His disciples the Lord's prayer, Jesus told them not to do that. He said, "But when you pray, do not use vain repetitions as the heathen do. For they think they will be heard for their many words" (Matthew 6:7 – The Open Bible).

A true disciple of Christ installs knowing and doing God's will at the top of his chart. Submission to Jesus as Lord and Savior requires nothing less. Doing the Father's will was certainly the mission of His life on earth, and what He expects of His followers.

What is God's will? Phillip Keller answers that question by saying, "To make the subject of God, our Father's will, as simple as possible, it is helpful first to realize what it is. The will of God is simply God's intentions. It is what He purposes. It is what He plans and wants to be done."

How extensive is God's will? What areas of my life does it affect? And where do I find it? Phillip Keller says, "God's will penetrates every area of life. . . It is so all-pervading it even finds an outlet in the details of day-to-day decisions which Christ's followers make for His sake. . . Through His written word, we can obtain very clear and explicit concepts of what He wants. . . This applies to every area of our lives, be it physical, moral, spiritual, or even in our careers."

He elaborates further by saying, "It is often mistakenly thought that the will of God, as in the Ten Commandments of Exodus 20, constitute His entire code of conduct for our lives. This is not so. For example, there are numerous passages throughout the Bible which give us clear and explicit instructions about such everyday matters as what we should eat; what we should drink; how we should think; how we should exercise; how we should work; how we should handle our money; how we should treat our wives, husbands, children, and parents. We are even instructed on such subjects as law and order, paying taxes, borrowing and lending, debts, hospitality, talking too much, as well as beneficial and wholesome sex." [5]

This all-pervading guidance has not been given by our Creator for our detriment, unnecessary restriction, deprivation, or any other negative reason. On the contrary, He made us and knows what's best for us to function at peak efficiency; how we can be contented and fulfilled in this life; what allows us to live harmoniously with others and all elements of society; how to prosper in spirit, soul and body while on this earth. Those who study the Bible consistently and apply it in a practical manner readily admit that God's way is far superior to man's way in all aspects of life. To put it bluntly, it works!

Acquiring Knowledge

In contrast to Hosea's pronouncement of destruction upon those lacking in knowledge repeated earlier in this chapter, the prophet Isaiah describes the effect of God's glory upon His people. While he speaks to the nation of Israel, all who submit to Jesus as Lord and Savior can receive encouragement from the following passage. Speaking for God, Isaiah said, " 'As for me, this is my covenant with them,' says the Lord. 'My Spirit, who is on you, and my words that I have put in your mouth will not depart from your mouth, or from the mouths of your children, or from the mouths of their descendants from this time on and forever,' says the Lord.

"ARISE, SHINE, for your light has come, and the glory of the Lord rises upon you. See, darkness covers the earth and thick darkness is over the peoples, but the Lord rises upon you and his glory appears over you" (Isaiah 59:21 and 60:1,2).

Don't miss the contrast here. When God's people lack or reject scriptural knowledge, both they and their children are destroyed. But when His Word abides in their hearts and fills their mouth, His blessings are upon them and their descendants. Ignorance and/or disobedience of God's will and way is synonymous to darkness, while knowledge and obedience allows the light of God's presence to penetrate and fill one's mind and heart. Did you know the source of the well-worn expression, "Arise and Shine!"? Do you understand what's required for attaining the ability to respond to that command?

Paul instructed his disciple Timothy to "Study to show thyself approved unto God, a workman that needeth not to be ashamed, rightly dividing the word of truth" (2 Timothy 2:15 – KJV). The word study is commonly defined as reading so as to understand and remember; to carefully think about, examine or investigate for the purpose of learning. Reading is the first of the three Rs, and in fact the only real one. But let's disregard the spelling issue, and hear what the Reverend Charles Swindoll has to say on the topic of reading.

"The three Rs have stood the test of time as reliable criteria for a dependable education. They are poised like disciplined sentinels against one of man's greatest enemies: ignorance. The original blocks of granite, unimpressed by educational styles, unmoved by change, these three solid friends are trustworthy to the end. Like salve on an open sore, they reduce the fever of panic, giving stability when so many voices demand obedience.

"But there is a fly in the ointment. . . one chunk of granite is beginning to crack. . . the sentinel is getting sleepy. The enemy has found the chink in our armor. He has discovered that the first "R" is up for grabs in the twentieth century. And he is smiling.

" 'Send me a man who reads' is no longer the clarion call of industry or management. . . or sales, for that matter. Nor is the professional person necessarily known today, as he once was, for his breadth of knowledge. . . and that includes (much to my disappointment) the clergy."

Pastor Swindoll goes on to provide alarming facts about the lack of reading done by college graduates in general; and doctors, lawyers and others we must depend upon for professional help and technical advice in particular. He speaks of second and third graders who struggle with their primary reader, yet knew the day, hour and channel for a dozen different TV programs prior to attending school. Many parents have apparently abdicated their responsibility to supplement the teaching their children receive in school, allowing television to do it for them.

Pastor Swindoll concludes this particular dissertation by providing four benefits of reading:

"1. Reading sweeps the cobwebs away.

"It enhances thinking. It stretches and strains our mental muscles. It clobbers our brittle, narrow, intolerant opinions with new ideas and strong facts. It stimulates growing up instead of growing old.

"Bacon's famous rule is true, so good: Read not to contradict or confute, nor to believe and take for granted, nor to find talk and discourse, but to weigh and consider. Some books are to be tasted, others to be swallowed, and some few to be chewed and digested.

"Reading expands us. It scratches those itches down deep inside. It navigates us through virgin territory we would not otherwise explore.

"2. Reading increases our power of concentration.

"Through this discipline, the mind is programmed to observe and absorb. It replaces the 'Entertain Me' mentality with 'Challenge Me.' The eye of a reader is keen, alert, probing, questioning.

"3. Reading makes us more interesting to be around.

"Small wonder the boredom factor in social gatherings is so great! After you've run through the weather, the kids, the job, and your recent surgery, what else is there? Being a reader adds oil to the friction in conversation. Furthermore, it opens to the Christian new avenues of approach in evangelism. It helps to meet the lost on their own ground and have them realize that becoming a Christian isn't like committing intellectual suicide. We need to read widely, including some periodicals as well as the classics.

"4. Reading strengthens our ability to glean truth from God's Word." [6]

It's here that Pastor Swindoll stops building his case for reading. He simply quotes 2 Timothy 4:13 -- the passage where Paul instructs his disciple Timothy to come quickly and bring his coat and books, especially the books. Keep in mind that Paul was writing from the dungeon, awaiting martyrdom. This great saint lived what he preached -- "Study to show yourself approved unto God."

A wise proverb states, "I hear and I forget; I see and I remember; I do and I understand." Researchers claim we retain 10% of what we hear, 50% of what we see, and 90% of what we do." It is my observation that those with good reading habits progress in their walk with the Lord to a far greater extent than those who mostly or solely listen to teaching/preaching tapes and Christian broadcasting. This, I believe, has to do with visual focus.

It is said "the eyes are the windows of the soul" – the mind, emotions and will.

Focusing on the printed page permits that which is found there to enter the mind and be considered there. If it's met with approval and comprehension, it stirs the emotions and is applied by the will.

On the other hand, that which the eyes focus on while listening to tapes compete for the individual's attention. So use your available study time wisely and read whatever promotes your knowledge of God's Word, way and will.

Chapter Thirteen Consequences of Ignorance or Disobedience of God s Word

Earlier in this chapter, we discussed the need to know God's law, preach repentance, and avoid the consequences of a lawless gospel. I read about a frontier town where a horse bolted and ran away with a wagon carrying a little boy. Seeing the child in danger, a young man risked his life to catch the horse and stop the wagon.

The child who was saved grew up to become a lawless man, and one day he stood before a judge to be sentenced for a serious crime. The prisoner recognized the judge as the man who, years ago, had saved his life; so he pled for mercy on the basis of that experience. But the words from the bench silenced his plea:

"Young man, then I was your savior, today I am your judge; and I must sentence you to be hanged." *

Need I say more?

The Safe Path in a Dangerous World

Being an overcomer throughout this life, whether times are tough or otherwise, is a difficult assignment indeed. Depending on your temperament, degree of personal confidence, resolve developed over the years, and existing spiritual, mental, emotional, physical and material resources, there is some force of nature relentlessly applied against you.

Some have never denied their carnal appetites. They can't seem to get off the merry-go-round of Sin and Repent; Sin and Repent. Others are timid and forever wanting to give up and give in to the fear of the unknown. They tend to tuck and hide, refusing to take any risk or allow themselves to be vulnerable. Some find it difficult to be content with who they are and what they have. They are forever tempted to stray from their vows, commitments and responsibilities to seek greener pastures. Still others want to grab all this world seems to offer while seeking God's approval and blessings on all their efforts. They lean towards straddling the picket fence with one foot on the temporal and the other on the eternal, knowing that a debilitating slip may be just one step away. All of us who profess belief and trust in Christ have a battle of some type on our hands.

The psalmist, in that wonderful – though lengthy – Psalm 119, provides us with what's essential for fighting the good fight and never giving in or giving up. It's the compass and map I turn to when I feel confused or lost. I would hope you make that your practice each time you feel weak, or are tempted to quit, stray, or compromise your integrity.

A portion of it says, "How can a young man keep his way pure? By living according to your word. I seek you with all my heart; do not let me stray from your commands. I have hidden your word in my heart that I might not sin against you" (9-11).

Truth is a marvelous thing. I love it because it is always there; is consistent and reliable; does not dry up or decay; is not contingent on human approval nor affected by popular opinion; and it functions according to its God-ordained decrees regardless of opposing circumstances or dispositions. I don't need to know, believe or agree with it for it to have its way. But if I do know it and choose to comply with it, I will be transported to where it travels. And since truth is created and energized by God, I am assured that both the trip and its destination is His best for me. So knowing the truth and living accordingly is of the utmost importance to disciples of Christ.

Hypothetical Situation

Here's a fictional account of how a lack of knowledge can destroy you physically. Imagine for a moment that you have spent the past few hours riding your motorcycle through the peace and splendor of a large rural segment of one of our western states. You are engrossed with nature's awesome beauty, paying little attention to the many turns taken. Suddenly an ominous sign informs you that the area you're in has been contaminated by a malfunction at the nearby nuclear power plant. You have no compass or map, and could not possibly retrace your trail. So what should you do?

If you are a consistent reader, always probing for awareness and understanding of the facts of life, you may have stumbled on an article about the nuclear disaster occurring on 4/26/86 in Chernobyl of the then crumbling Soviet Union.

If so, you would know that the lowest level of radiation in the area would be found in the middle of its asphalt roads. It would be twice as high at either edge of the road, and four or five times higher immediately off the road. That's because radiation sits on the soil, grass, apples, mushrooms and all other vegetation. It is not retained by asphalt. And since there are no moving objects around to stir up the dust, you might just escape serious harm by staying in "the middle of the

111

road." Isn't that usually the safest place, out of reach of the devil that roams about as a tethered lion wanting to devour all who depart from the Lord's way and will? But knowledge and discipline are essential to find and remain in that sheltered place.

Conclusion

Sound logic and positive encouragement works for most of us, but some are moved only by fear. To those I offer Pastor John Hagee's vivid description of knowledge void of God's truth. In his Beginning Of The End, he briefly details the phenomenal scientific achievements over the past century, then says, "All this knowledge ought to be a good thing, but still we're on the road to Armageddon. Our knowledge has not produced utopia; instead it has created a generation of well-informed people who know more about rock stars than history. Our "enlightened" society seeks freedom and self-expression, but is actually enslaved by drugs, perversion, and occult practices.

"We favor death for the innocent and mercy for the guilty. We tout the benefits of secular humanism, the worship of man's intellect, yet our enlightened, religion-free government finds itself impotent in the face of growing crime. Why? Because knowledge without God can only produce intellectual barbarians, smarter sinners. Hitler's Nazis threw Jewish children alive into the ovens. Many of them were educated men, some had Ph.D's, but their education was accomplished without the acknowledgment or the knowledge of God.

"We are the terminal generation, 'always learning but never able to come to the knowledge of the truth' (2 Timothy 3:7) because we seek truth apart from God. You can't think your way to truth. You can't philosophize your way there. You can't think happy thoughts and find truth. The only way you will ever find eternal, ultimate truth, is by seeking and finding God.

"If you reject truth, the only thing left to accept is a lie. America has rejected the truth of God's Word. We have rejected God Himself, and all we have left is the secular humanist lie. But Jesus said, 'You shall know the truth, and the truth shall make you free' (John 8:32)." [7]

So add knowledge to goodness, but be sure it's based on truth.

Lesson Six
Add self-control To Knowledge

SELF-CONTROL IS SELF-DENIAL, personal discipline and more. 2 Peter 1 says we must add self-control to faith, goodness and knowledge to escape the corruption in the world caused by evil desires.

Unbridled anger and its varying forms of expression is, for many, the most destructive force within their lives. Temper, when judiciously applied for a righteous cause, can strengthen one's position for solving problems and achieving goals. So don't lose it. All who allow this consuming fire to rage at will are assured of failure, misery, and physical and emotional bankruptcy. The principal of self-control contains lessons of patience, purity, gentleness, kindness and steadfastness. These can only be learned slowly, but until they are, a person's success and character remain uncertain. For when our thoughts, words, actions and reactions are ordered by a healthy spirit, mind and attitude, our course is no longer charted by conditions , circumstances and contemporaries. Henry Emerson Fosdick said, "No horse gets anywhere until it is harnessed. No life ever grows great until it is focussed, dedicated, disciplined." And that requires self-control .

To avoid confusion, let's distinguish between what is self-control and what is not. Weak individuals allow their mental energy to fall into the safe and easy channels of least resistance. They profess opinions that are popular, and take risk-free positions on all controversial issues. Those who exercise self-control, on the other hand, gain power by gathering, focussing and forcing their mental energies into upward and difficult directions.

Some are deluded into thinking that the smothering and hiding of one's true nature for no higher purpose than to create a good impression is self-control. It is not. That is hypocrisy. For one who practices self-control performs a task similar to those who convert coal and water into energy for the purpose of concentrating and utilizing those forces to enhance man's comfort and convenience. A similar thing occurs when one diligently overcomes his own base nature by converting his lower inclinations into the finer qualities of intelligence and morality to heighten his and others' happiness and contentment.

Chapter Fourteen An Essential Element of Freedom

Proponents of our permissive and defiled culture announce that true freedom results only when individuals pursue the fulfillment of their sensual desires and personal gratification. All inhibitions and moral restraints are denounced as joy and happiness killers. They say, "If you want it, take it." "If it feels good, do it." "If it pleases your senses, it's wrong and foolish to deny yourself that pleasure."

God's Word and life's experiences say otherwise. Such conduct destroys our important relationships. It creates serious conflicts by interfering with, intruding on or invading what belongs to another. Bondage, rather than freedom, results when one is enslaved by his own lusts, greed or wicked desires.

A fourteenth century duke in what is now Belgium, named Raynald III, was grossly overweight. His nickname was Crassus, meaning "fat." After a violent quarrel, his younger brother Edward led a revolt against Raynald. He captured him and imprisoned him in Nieuwkerk Castle by building a room around him. It contained an unlocked door and unbarred windows of near normal size. Edward promised Raynald his freedom and the return of his title whenever he was able to leave the room.

The devious younger brother, however, sent a variety of delicious foods to Raynald's room every day knowing he was incapable of denying himself of such delicacies. As a result, he grew even larger and all the more unable to squeeze through the door or windows.

Raynald remained in that room for ten years until Edward was killed in battle and a wall of that room removed. By then he was in ill health and died within a year. His lack of self-control made him a prisoner of his own appetite. *

The Control Issue

Control means to have power or authority to rule, guide or manage. It can be used either positively or negatively. The Bible instructs us to use our God-given power or authority to nurture, encourage, and lead others to Him. Many, however, use it to manipulate, intimidate or deceive the weak and subordinate for selfish purposes or nefarious gratification.

Leaders of the world's religions often exercise control over their membership by exhorting submission to the sect's behavior code in order to earn God's approval and deserve salvation, or what is thought to be its equivalent. Buddhists have their Eight-Fold Path, Hindus their doctrine of Karma, Jews their Covenant, Muslims their Code of Law, and Roman Catholics their Works-Righteousness doctrinal system.

Biblical Christianity, which is a relationship and not a religion, dares to make God's love unconditional. It is best defined as a Justification by Grace Alone Through Faith Alone doctrinal system. It teaches that salvation is based solely on Christ's work on the cross, and that Scripture alone is wholly sufficient for the establishment and understanding of all we need to know to please God and spend eternity with Him.

The problem is, however, that man's nature requires him to be in control, or at least think he is. The idea of God's love being available free of charge with no strings attached arouses his suspicions and invalidates the pride he desires to experience from earning God's favor. But self-control empowers the disciples of Christ to accept the fact that we humans cannot ascend to God, and thus become eternally grateful that He was willing to come down to us.

Self-control is likewise essential within the Reformers' Individual Priesthood of the Believer principle which makes each child of God responsible for what he believes and how he lives in accordance with those beliefs. He must refuse to compromise his integrity, resist the ever-present pressure to re-take control of his own life, and daily submit to the lordship of Jesus. He must also be vigilant in resisting the practices taught by false teachers who pervert Scripture and proclaim that through the extraordinary use of faith, one can actually control God. But that, my friend, is the deadly sin of presumption.

I read of a woman who was married for many years to a harsh and controlling man who daily left her a list of chores he expected to be completed prior to his return from work. Failure to meet his demands evoked his anger and demeaning temperament. But even when all listed tasks were performed, he found fault in her work. The woman suffered from depression, chronic anxiety, guilt and feelings of inadequacy as a result of this relationship.

The husband died in middle-age, and his widow eventually re-married. This time she chose a kind and tender man who lavished her with praise and appreciation. One day while cleaning out a box of old papers, she discovered one of her first husband's task lists. A tear of joy fell to the paper when she realized she continued to do all of those things. But she no longer did them because it was demanded or expected of her. She did them willingly and without being asked, simply because she loved the man who treated her well.

The woman's two husbands define the difference between religion and Christianity. Jesus denounced the Jewish leaders for laying a burden upon their people that they, themselves, would not, could not, bear. In his book Guilt and Grace, the Swiss doctor Paul Tournier said, "I cannot study this very serious problem of guilt with you without raising the very obvious and tragic fact that religions – my own as well as that of all believers – can crush instead of liberate." (1)

Jesus, on the other hand, came as a light into this dark world to set us captives free, so that we may have life and have it more abundantly. Those who exercise self-control in accordance with God's Word need never submit to the control of religious folks with their pernicious rules, regulations and decrees.

The humorist Erma Bombeck illustrated this stark difference beyond my capacity to describe it. She wrote, "In church the other Sunday I was intent on a small child who was turning around smiling at everyone. He wasn't gurgling, spitting, humming, kicking, tearing the hymnals, or rummaging through his mother's handbag. He was just smiling. Finally, his mother jerked him about and in a stage whisper that could be heard in a little theater off Broadway said, 'Stop that grinning! You're in church!' With that, she gave him a belt and as the tears rolled down his cheeks added, 'That's better,' and returned to her prayers. . .

"Suddenly I was angry. It occurred to me the entire world is in tears, and if you're not, then you'd better get with it. I wanted to grab this child with the tear-stained face close to me and tell him about my God. The happy God. The smiling God. The God who had to have a sense of humor to have created the likes of us. . . By tradition, one wears faith with the solemnity of a mourner, the gravity of a mask of tragedy, and the dedication of a Rotary badge.

"What a fool, I thought. Here was a woman sitting next to the only light left in our civilization--the only hope, our only miracle--our only promise of infinity. If he couldn't smile in church, where was there left to go?" [1]

Use The Forces at Work

A delightful book entitled Prime Time was written awhile back by the Reverend Herb Barks. He speaks in there about his interest in riding the rapids down the Chattanooga River. A professional guide saw his love for the river and encouraged him to learn how to use its power. He taught him to stop fighting it and flow with the current.

"I had listened to my culture," said Pastor Barks at this point, "and bought the pattern of competitiveness, tenseness, achievement, pain, and in doing so I had lost some of the joy of living." He talks about how the frantic race and pace of our materialistic striving have driven many of our citizens to the Eastern practices of Zen, meditation and yoga. Instead of sitting cross-legged to observe a flower, Reverend Barks says we need only listen to and obey the Lord.

Jesus said, "So do not worry, saying, 'What shall we eat?' or 'What shall we drink?' or 'What shall we wear?' For the pagans run after all these things, and your heavenly Father knows that you need them. But seek first his kingdom and his righteousness, and all these things will be given to you as well" (Matthew 6:31-33).

That should get our attention. The Lord is telling us to stop pursuing that which nonbelievers seek continuously – more, more, more. We should have a totally different agenda. As elaborated upon in the previous chapter, learning and doing God's will should be our passion and purpose. But Pastor Barks is right when he says this requires an all new mind-set.

He says, "What Jesus is saying to me is that I should quit worrying about fighting life, about paddling fiercely down a raging river. Instead I should get in touch with the power of the water and let it carry me. Birds and flowers are not striving to achieve flight or buds; they just fly and grow."

He's talking about that control issue we just discussed. The Lord is telling us in the above passage to dare to loosen our grip and permit Him to love and lead us; provide for and protect us; unburden and use us for kingdom purposes. We need to slow down to see what God wants to do in our lives; be still and hear what His Spirit is saying to our hearts. It's a conscious and deliberate choice we need to make.

Pastor Barks speaks to the crew in his boat: "I tell them that brute strength isn't what counts. The river is too powerful to even consider strength against it. What is important is rhythm and timing, and position, using the forces already at work.

"And Jesus says exactly the same thing to me. He says, 'Don't thrash around. You must allow the power to flow through you, to open yourself to the power of love.' I am trying to be the tractor while He wants me to be the plow. He will supply the power. What a relief it is if I don't have to make it happen, but can let it happen."

He admits that it sounds much easier than it is. Most of us have spent years of our lives doing things the world's way. And the voices and visions all around us insist there is no other logical mode of living. This vital change in our thinking, speaking and acting won't happen without dedication and determination.

In reference to Matthew 6:33, Pastor Barks says, "What this means to me is that I can stop seeking all of the world's prizes, stop seeking all the material security, and instead decide to live as a channel – care about relationships first and to make love the central issue of my life. I can choose to live a day at a time, letting each day take care of itself, finding some way to love somebody, and out of that to discover who I was meant to be. . .

"I feel that the world around me and the culture in which I live has taught me the wrong way to live. I need a new decision about life that will free me up to run with life rather than to fight against it. . . Try to develop the skill of flowing with life. It is not what we achieve that counts; it is who we are for Him. It is how we have tapped into the power that flows beside us and beneath us. We can't survive by struggling against His power, against His will for us. We can wear ourselves out paddling for the glitter of this world. And all the time His will for us is to let Him surge under our boat and take us where He would." [2]

The Apostle Peter's recommended progression for partaking of the divine nature reflects his understanding of human nature. First we must trust solely in God and not ourselves. Then we must work towards becoming a person of integrity and perfecting our character. Then we must learn all we can about God and His will for our individual life, and how it differs from man's way of doing and being. Then we must choose to change, and exercise self-control in carrying out that important decision.

Chapter Fifteen We Must Be Diligent

England's famous 19th century evangelist, Charles Haddon Spurgeon, denounced believers who wasted and forfeited their walk with the Lord due to laziness. In his Words Of Wisdom For Daily Living, he says, "A man cannot be idle and yet have Christ's sweet company. Christ is a quick walker. When His people want to talk with Him, they must also travel quickly, or else they will soon lose His company. Christ, my Master, goes about doing good, and if you would walk with Him you must go about upon the same mission. The Almighty lover of the souls of men does not want to keep company with idle persons.

"I find in Scripture that most of the great appearances that were made to eminent saints were made when they were busy. Moses was tending his father-in-law's flock when he saw the burning bush. Joshua was going around about the city of Jericho when he met the angel of the Lord. Jacob was in prayer and the angel of God appeared to him. Gideon was threshing, and Elisha was plowing, when the Lord called them. Matthew was collecting customs when he was bidden to follow Jesus, and James and John were fishing. The manna which the children of Israel kept until morning bred worms and stank. Idle grace would soon become active corruption.

"Moreover, sloth hardens the conscience. Laziness is one of the irons with which the heart is seared. Abimelech hired vain, light persons to serve his turn, and the prince of darkness does the same. Friends, it is a sad thing to rust the edge off from one's mind and to lose keenness of moral perception, but sloth will surely do this for us. . .

"Some temptations come to the industrious, but all temptations attack the idle. Notice the invention used by country people to catch wasps. They will put a little sweet liquor into a long, narrow-necked vial. The do-nothing wasp comes by, smells the sweet liquor, plunges in, and is drowned. But the bee comes by, and, if she does stop for a moment to smell, yet she does not enter because she has honey of her own to make. She is too busy in the work of the commonwealth to indulge herself with the tempting sweets."[3]

David's son Solomon saw idleness in a similar manner, describing it as follows: "I went past the field of the slothful, past the vineyard of the man who lacks judgment; thorns had come up everywhere, the ground was covered with weeds, and the stone wall was in ruins. I applied my heart to what I observed and learned a lesson from what I saw; a little sleep, a little slumber, a little folding of the hands to rest – and poverty will come on you like a bandit and scarcity like an armed man" (Prov. 24:30-34).

With this in mind, know that there is a thief in each of our homes. Nothing so defrauds our time, desensitizes our spirit, debilitates our mind, and destroys our body like the boob tube. And what portion of our spare time the TV doesn't steal, the computer aggressively pursues. Even if you watch nothing but sports, in the course of a professional football game you generally see a half dozen commercials selling computers, software products and internet services. Those who resist their enticements are made to fear they will fail in the market place, fall short at home, and die with many unresolved issues because they rejected this information storehouse.

Those who buy it all and spend endless at-home hours on their computer may succeed in some financial endeavors. Even that, however, is no guarantee as most of those filing for bankruptcy these days have ownership of, or at least access to, plenty of computer equipment. But failure in their marriage and the raising of their children is certainly enhanced. And believers who are deceived into thinking that the internet can answer all their questions and solve all their problems, won't waste valuable on-line time studying Scripture or in prayer.

Jesus said, "Do not love the world or anything in the world. If anyone loves the world, the love of the Father is not in him. For everything in the world – the cravings of sinful man, the lust of the eyes and the boasting of what he has and does – comes not from the Father but from the world. The world and its desires pass away, but the man who does the will of God lives forever" (1 John 2:15-17).

The will of God is to be a good steward of all that He has given you. Show your appreciation for Him sacrificing His only begotten Son to secure your Salvation by communing daily with Him in Bible study and prayer. Demonstrate your love for Him by obeying his Word in all aspects of your life in accordance with instructions found in John's gospel. Cherish the spouse He provided by spending quality time each day nurturing her or him as Jesus nurtures His church. Love, guard, guide, discipline and enjoy those precious gifts of life He presented to both of you. Be diligent in the exercise and care of the physical body the Lord gave you, and properly maintain all of His material blessings. And when all of that has been achieved in addition to working hard at the job He provided, there will be no time or energy for that which steals and destroys.

This is good advice, but without self-control it won't be heeded. Deny yourself of that which displeases the Lord. Discipline yourself in His way. And exercise proper control over all He has placed in your care.

Refuse to Compromise

A high school biology class put a frog in a large pot of water with no lid, and over a very low fire. It was quite comfortable and felt no need to jump out.

The water heated slowly, but the change was so gradual that the frog didn't notice. The steadily warming water relaxed the animal, causing it to become lethargic. By the time the temperature of the water became uncomfortable, the frog's strength, energy and ability to jump out of the pot had dissipated.

Nothing but its unawareness of the danger it faced kept that frog in harm's way. It was comfortable, dropped its guard, became complacent and got cooked.

The word compromise has a dual meaning; one part positive and the other negative. The latter part defines the willingness to jeopardize my walk with the Lord, the relationship with my spouse and children, and my reputation as a man of integrity for a moment's pleasure or a financial advantage. This is foolish and should be avoided.

The experimental frog exhibited the essence of the negative side of compromise as well as its consequences. He epitomizes the fool in Proverbs 14:16 which says, "A wise man is cautious and avoids danger, but a fool throws off restraint and is careless." When we venture where wise men fear to tread, we inevitably end up in hot water.

Guard The Back Door

A quaint story found in an old Spanish text book tells of a lonely stretch of mountain road where a traveler met the devil one day. The terrified man tried in vain to step around the evil one. The devil laughed at the traveler's pleas to allow him to pass, saying that would occur only when he promised to do one of three things.

The man flatly refused the first option which was to kill his beloved wife of many years. And he likewise vigorously rejected the second choice which was to drive from home the children he delighted in. But to bring the unpleasant confrontation to a quick end, he submitted to the devil's third proposal and drank the cask of wine he offered.

Now that his state of mind and heart were altered, he was permitted to continue on. He arrived home shortly thereafter, killed his wife and drove away his children. [4]

The traveler unfortunately didn't know the biblical admonition to "Therefore submit to God. Resist the devil and he will flee from you" (James 4:7). And he obviously had not taken Paul's advice to "Put on the full armor of God so that you can take your stand against the devil's schemes" (Ephesians. 6:11). The tempter knows human nature well. If a believer diligently locks the front door to blatant sin, Satan will knock on the back door with subtle temptation and compromise.

God always provides an evacuation route from temptation (1 Cor. 10:13), but we must want to take it. The better way, however, is to keep out of that pot to begin with. Honor your marriage vows and esteem the mate God gave you by keeping all others at "arm's length." Avoid all pornography, "hard" or "soft," and books that stir your passion and encourage fantasy pondering. Establish and maintain an agreement with your spouse that no impure literature nor movies rated lower than "P-G" enter your home. Guard your thoughts, words and ways daily so that no time nor energy is wasted on running from what should never get near you.

An American professor named Joseph Fletcher published an influential book in

1966 called Situation Ethics. His basic premise was that there are no absolutes; nothing is universally good or bad, right or wrong; morals are determined by the situation.

This cancer began as a philosophical discussion, but has rapidly spread throughout our land producing a moral and ethical crisis reaching epidemic proportions. Prior to that time, our country followed the Judeo-Christian ethic based on the absolutes of Scripture.

Despite what goes on all around you, follow the advice offered by a particular bumper sticker. It said, "Live your life in such a way so the good preacher won't have to lie at your funeral."

Control Your Body

Chapter two dealt solely with the physiology aspects of the body; the need to understand how it functions and what it requires. Now we must focus on the sensual features of the body; those which respond to sights, sounds, smells, touches and tastes. Physical fitness demands we give the body what it needs; virtue dictates we constrain what it wants.

This paradox appears to be the cause of the Church's neglect relative to the proper care and maintenance of our temple of the Holy Spirit. Since much time and energy is expended on repairing the damage reaped by the sowing of undisciplined sensuality, the Christian community struggles to believe the body has a good side. Exercising self-control over our carnal appetites is thus essential for attaining and maintaining spirit, soul and body fitness.

In his letter to the church at Philippi, Paul said, "Therefore, my dear friends, as you have always obeyed – not only in my presence, but now much more in my absence – continue to work out your salvation with fear and trembling, for it is

God who works in you to will and act according to his good purpose" (Philippians 2:12,13). Proponents of Works Righteousness, Conditional Security and Eternal Security all use, abuse or ignore this passage to promote their own doctrinal position. But I believe Paul is simply stating that Salvation is a process, not a do-it and forget-it event. He encouraged believers in Christ to never give-in or let-up against the evil forces that oppose each of us all the time. And he reminds the reader of their need of God's help and presence to achieve this victory.

The December 5th devotion in Oswald Chambers' My Utmost For His Highest speaks of how we must account to God for the manner in which we rule our body. He stresses our responsibility to exercise dominion over our imaginations and affections. [5]

Properly responding to the tough times that await us, as well as those presently upon us, require a high level of readiness. That is a full-time, all-the-time job demanding faith, goodness, knowledge and self-control.

Lesson Seven
Add Perseverance to Self-Control

MANY YEARS AGO IN A QUAINT European farming community, two young brothers stole sheep from neighbors rather than earning a living by hard work. They were eventually caught and ST was branded on their foreheads. There were no jails in the area, so the authorities chose this method for warning residents that Sheep Thieves were among them.

One of the young men could not deal with the humiliation and stigmatized mark. He left that part of the country and was never heard from again.

The other one decided to humbly confront his errant ways and earn the respect and trust of his neighbors. That wasn't easy. He had to live with their scorn and rejection, and work long and tedious hours for meager wages. Despite all of that, he made himself readily available during his free time to help those in need.

His perseverance and sincerity wore down his neighbors' resistance, and in due time he became one of the most respected and trusted residents of that village. While dining in an outdoor restaurant one day, a visitor asked the owner what the ST meant that was branded on the forehead of the gentleman sitting in the corner and getting all the attention. "I'm not sure," replied the proprietor, "but I think it means saint." [1]

The apostle Peter tells us in 2 Peter 1:6 to add perseverance to self-control in our efforts to keep from being ineffective and unproductive in our knowledge of our Lord Jesus Christ. That's not a popular trait in our fast food and instant gratification culture.

Who wants to stick to a task or purpose until it's properly completed despite difficulties and problems encountered during the process? Who wants to be patient and persistent until relationships are healed or conditions improve? Who wants to ask and keep on asking until it is given; seek and keep on seeking until it is found; knock and keep on knocking until the door opens? (Matthew 7:7) I thought I had a right to what I want, when I want it, without working up a sweat. Could our contemporary society be giving us the wrong message?

The above story conveys perseverance beyond my capacity to explain it. God's way of righting wrongs, resolving disputes, and receiving His guidance and blessings is to just keep on keeping on until the Lord's plan and purpose is performed. The Bible tells us, "Hezekiah trusted in the Lord, the God of Israel. There was no one like him among all the kings of Judah, either before him or after him. He held fast to the Lord and did not cease to follow Him; he kept the commands the Lord had given Moses. And the Lord was with him; he was successful in whatever he undertook" (2 Kings 18:5-7).

Chapter Sixteen Wait Upon The Lord

One of the first Scriptures to excite me shortly after submitting my life to Christ in 1975 was Proverbs 4:18. This verse says, "The path of the righteous is like the first light of dawn, shining ever brighter until the full light of day." The Living Bible paraphrase says it this way: "But the good man walks along in the ever-brightening light of God's favor."

I was a young husband and father at the time, forever consumed by fears and anxieties. My life was not getting progressively better, and the storm cloud hovering overhead insisted it wouldn't. I learned that righteous means just; remaining faithful to God and one's spouse; meeting the standard of life prescribed by the Lord in His Word. So if I wanted this promise to be true, I knew I had to become righteous.

I believed then, and still do after years of indisputable evidence, that traveling on an ever-brightening path during this life is a possibility. It requires submission to Jesus as Lord and Savior; knowledge of and consistent obedience to God's word; trusting the Lord to keep His promises; and waiting on Him to intervene and intercede on our behalf.

There's the rub; the fly in the ointment if you will. Waiting on God to act on our behalf is essential for experiencing this promise, and that opposes our nature.

We may give God a few days, a week, or perhaps a month. But then we take matters into our own hands while expecting Him to bless our efforts. Take it from one who's been there, done that – it doesn't work.

Psalm 37 tells us what is essential for walking along in the ever-brightening light of God's favor. It says, "Trust in the Lord and do good; dwell in the land and enjoy safe pasture. Delight yourself in the Lord and he will give you the desires of your heart. Commit your way to the Lord; trust in him and he will do this: He will make your righteousness shine like the dawn, the justice of your cause like the noonday sun. Be still before the Lord and wait patiently for him; do not fret when men succeed in their ways, when they carry out their wicked schemes. . .

"Wait for the Lord and keep his way. He will exalt you to possess the land; when the wicked are cut off, you will see it" (Psalm 37: 3-7 and 34).

It Requires Tenacity

That passage illustrates the two aspects of perseverance. The first is to refuse to compromise your integrity and persist in learning, doing and responding God's way despite no apparent change or improvement in your circumstances, relationships, etc. The second is to resist capitulating to impatience by trying to make things happen; giving in to the absurd notion that the Lord needs our help to bring about His purposes.

The spirit, soul and body must all be actively engaged here. Our spirit perceives and believes that the invisible God wrote that Book and will do what He promised therein if we do as He instructs. As for our soul, we must be mentally alert to what transpires, maintain emotional stability and persistently submit our will to God's will. And our physical, sensual being must be disciplined and deny its desires when they conflict with the Lord's. Hold on to the hope that in due time as promised in Psalm 37:34, "you will see it."

A man who loved nature and the freedom of the outdoors applied for an exciting job with the forestry service. He was given a 4:00 P.M. appointment on a particular Monday during December. The interview was scheduled to take place at a lookout post on top of a nearby mountain inundated with snow.

There was over 200 applicants for this interesting position. Each of them received the same interview appointment time at the same location. This man was the only one to arrive for the assigned conference. He got the job and enjoyed it for many years..

It Takes Time

A couple and their son, Junior, had spent their entire lives in the back hills of West Virginia. They didn't own a television, had no access to a movie theater, and had never been to a big city. The bright lights and modern inventions of a large metropolitan area were totally unknown to them.

As Junior reached his late teens, the father felt an obligation and responsibility to prepare his son for manhood. It troubled him that Junior may take a job in the city and be incapable of facing and dealing with the real world. So they saved and planned for a few days vacation in the big city.

The sights and sounds of the metropolis totally captivated them as they pulled up in front of a swanky hotel at which they chose to stay. Papa instructed mama to stay in the truck while he and Junior checked the place out.

Automatic doors, crystal chandeliers hanging from a ceiling 3 stories high, an enormous ornate waterfall, a long mall with many shops, and countless other visions had them staring in wide-eyed amazement. But a little room with doors that slid open from the center and flickering lights above them soon held their full attention. One group of people would walk up, push a button, and enter the room when the doors opened. The doors would close for a short while, and when they reopened a totally different looking group of people would exit.

Just then a wrinkled old lady shuffled up to the doors and pushed the button. As they opened, she entered the room alone and the doors closed. In just a few moments they re-opened, and there stood a beautiful and shapely young woman who smiled and walked out of the room and past them. Papa then nudged his boy and mumbled, "Quick, Junior. . . go git Mama!" [2]

Becoming Beautiful

It takes a long time to become beautiful. It doesn't just happen, and once it occurs we dare not get careless. True beauty requires ongoing maintenance and diligence.

To be beautiful, we have to be spiritually alive and vibrant. A close walk with the Lord keeps our fourth dimensional vision clear and sharp. It enables us to hear His voice, discern His purpose and follow His lead.

Our scriptural knowledge, comprehension and application must remain fresh and personal. It's essential that we present to the Lord a new wineskin each day -- one that is not stretched to capacity, dry and cracked. Only then can God pour into us the new wine of unique opportunities and experiences He has for us. This is what Jesus was trying to convey in Mark 2:22.

The Senate Chaplain, Pastor Lloyd John Ogilvie, teaches on this parable in his Autobiography Of God. He says, "A sure sign of a vital Christian is viability. He or she is open to grow and capable of freedom and flexibility. Faith is dynamic, not static. Fellowship with God is an adventure which is never completed. . . Whatever has happened to us is only a prelude to what God is about to do. . . We have hardly started to become the person He is ready and able to liberate us to be." (3)

Pastor Ogilvie reminds us that it's a human tendency to drop anchor at some point. We lose our excitement and enthusiasm for the new thing God wants to do in and through us. We become stale and satisfied with old experiences. We begin to lose our spiritual beauty. We must be always on guard against concluding that we are a finished product and need only repeat what we have done in the past.

To be beautiful, we must remain intellectually alert, active and honest. We should never rest on what we know, as a lifetime of learning absorbs but a small fragment of available knowledge. We must refuse to give yesterday's answers to today's questions, or resolve today's problems with yesterday's solutions.

We should search always for a broader perspective of what we already know. God has equipped each of us with a unique personality, temperament, burden and calling. We expand our own comprehension and approach to issues when we learn about that of others. And the Lord has provided a few with that special ability to challenge our thinking and help us probe a matter to a depth not previously attained. It's important to read their works and study their conclusions. They should be our mentors and guides.

The purpose is not to become like them or anyone else, but rather to maximize our own gifts and talents. This is why we must be intellectually honest. When we ask, "How does this apply to me?;" or "How can that improve my attitude or performance?;" or "What is the Lord trying to teach me here?;" we expand the path on which we are traveling.

We need not be afraid to expose our minds to new knowledge, opinions or ideas if we remain grounded in God's Word. His truth can be used to measure and test all things. We can always know what should be retained and applied; what should be stored away for future use; and what must be ignored or discarded. We are required to pick and choose, but it's essential that we never stop shopping.

To be beautiful, we must be genuinely interested in and concerned for others. Jesus said to His apostles on the night Judas betrayed Him, "A new command I give you: Love one another. As I have loved you, so you must love one another" (John 13:34). The love He spoke of has little in common with what poses as love in our self-centered society. It is not that which has no other purpose than to satisfy our own desires or relieve our insecurities. It is not that which involves a co-dependancy with another. And it is not that which is only given when specific conditions are met.

The love the Lord spoke of is that which desires God's best for another even when there's nothing in for me. It's that special way of extending ourselves so that others can become more of what God created them to be. It requires us to be vulnerable and risk being hurt or disappointed. It demands that we forego self-seeking and surrender to the Lord our personal agendas.

A passage in the Gospel of Matthew is very important to understand at this point. Jesus said, ". . .and love your neighbor as yourself" (Matthew 19:19). Our Creator understands our inability to care for another beyond our own feeling of self worth. That's why only those secure in God's love for themselves can truly love unconditionally. And that brings us back to the need to be spiritually, mentally and emotionally fit.

To be beautiful, the body God gave us must be well maintained. There's no requirement here to be a centerfold in a men's magazine nor on the cover of Muscle Beach Illustrated. That's impossible for most of us, and generally destructive for those with such physical attributes.

But it's important that we feel good about ourselves and make the best appearance possible. We profess to represent the King of kings and Lord of lords. Shouldn't that demand that we always look and feel our best? Doesn't that require us to be ready, willing and able to do what He sets before us; and keep on doing it long after everyone else has quit? Isn't life too short to run out of gas or wear out the tires before reaching our destination?

It takes muscles to live successfully during tough times – spiritual, mental, emotional and physical muscles. But muscles grow and develop slowly. They expand their capacity for action and achievement when new layers are continuously added. And that requires regular exercise and persistent rebuffing of the ever-present temptation to coast and compromise.

Chapter Seventeen Use Your Time wisely

If you have ever witnessed the damage to wooden structures caused by soft shell termites, it will help you understand what I've been saying. They come out of the ground, remain out of sight and work silently. These tiny white worms relentlessly devour everything in their path. If not stopped in time, they leave nothing but the outer shell. The slightest pressure then collapses the exterior and exposes the destruction.

Twenty-first century America's pampered, permissive society destroys our entire being if we don't repel it's obstinate seductions. Our post-Christian culture imposes upon us its secular, humanistic, new-age philosophy. And that will kill our spirit. In subtle and not so subtle ways, it attempts to do our thinking, establish our values and influence our attitudes. And that will kill our soul. Its various forms of media encourage us to maintain a frantic pace of never-ending acquisition of creature comforts, excessive possessions and devices that do most everything for us. And that will kill our body.

A somewhat new method for eradicating termites utilizes "bait stations." They are cylinders containing blocks of wood inserted in the ground at regular intervals surrounding the structure. The exterminator visits periodically, and exchanges the wood blocks for poison of equal consistency when the "bait" shows evidence of termite activity. The "worker" termites gnaw on the deadly chemical and take some back for the pleasure of the underground colony. While this process requires more time than the former method of injecting pesticides into the infected areas, no further damage is inflicted upon the building. And the underground members who produce the workers are eradicated along with them.

Achieving and maintaining spirit, soul and body fitness requires a similar method. all thought processes, attitudes, habits and life styles must be tested by God's Word and Holy Spirit discernment. Those that do not please the Lord nor enhance His plan and purpose for your life should be eradicated and replaced by those that lead to godly living.

A book entitled What Is Worthwhile, written during the late 1800s by Anna Robertson Brown, provides excellent guidance for helping us persevere in all of these areas. She asked five questions which challenge her readers to scrutinize the use of their time, energy and resources:

1) How can I accomplish the most with the energies and powers at my command?

2) What is worth the expending of those energies and powers?

3) What in life is worth holding onto?

4) What in life is vital?

5) What in life may I profitably let go of?

Ms. Brown followed-up her questions with four things that, when released, will unencumber our lives:

1) Drop pretense – Eternity is not for shams.

2) Don't worry – Placing too much value on small things is spiritual near-sightedness.

3) Let go of discontent – Be satisfied with and interested in whatever is set before us.   4) Let go of self-seeking – Eternal life contains no greed.

Developing character is a lifetime process. After asking her questions and suggesting four things of which to be released from, Anna Robertson Brown provided eight values which enhance one's life. They are:

1) Be wise in the use of the time God gives you.

2) Value work – Doing with all your might that which strengthens your character and   inspires or helps others.

3) Seek happiness each day by being patient, unselfish and purposeful with a grateful heart.

4) Cherish love – The true sort that neither nags nor tethers, but trusts and sets free.

5) Keep ambition in check by not allowing it to replace human affection.

6) Embrace friendship by forgiving, forgetting and forbearing much.

7) Do not fear sorrow as disappointment and pain is inevitable. And once you have   grieved, suffered and wept, you may help others who are in that process.

8) Cherish faith – Strong, serene and unquenchable faith in a loving, all-powerful God Who enables you to live this life effectively and grandly while awaiting fearlessly for the temporal to end and the eternal to begin. [4]

The author described herself as a lifelong student – one who is continually seeking knowledge in an effort to perceive the ultimate laws of god's universe. This is a wise manner in which to live one's life, and requires perseverance

Build Memorials

There are times in each of our lives when confusion reigns and everything around us seems to be crumbling. Things generally aren't as bad as they appear, but they will be if we panic and react on our fears. It's during those perilous times that we need to drop anchor until the storm works its way out of the area.

Psalm 125:1,2 tells us how to do that when it says, "THOSE WHO trust in the Lord are like Mount Zion, which cannot be shaken but endures forever. As the mountains surround Jerusalem, so the Lord surrounds his people both now and forevermore." So while we wait in a safe and serene place for the winds to subside, we should dwell on God's faithfulness to us in all such prior trials.

Our tendency is to keep so busy adding up our troubles, we forget to count our blessings. This is why we must, on occasion, set aside the present and reflect on the past. We may find that there were times when the Lord calmed the storm; and other times when He calmed us and let the storm raged. Either way, He brought us safely through it if we trusted Him to do so.

Man suffers from the old Out-of-Sight-Out-of-Mind Syndrome. For that reason, God required various memorials to be established in the form of special holy days, sacrificial practices, symbols on His priests' garments, and items within the tabernacle. These are found within the Mosaic Law and in the books of Exodus, Leviticus and Numbers. Each was in memory of a specific occasion when the mighty hand of God intervened on behalf of the nation of Israel to deliver them from Egypt's bondage, or to preserve them as they wandered forty years in the wilderness.

The Lord also instructed Joshua to remove twelve large stones from the midst of the Jordan River and erect them in Gilgal (Joshua 4). This was to remind all future generations within the Promised Land that God parted the waters of the Red Sea to allow Israel to escape from Pharaoh; and that He parted the Jordan River to bring that nation out of the wilderness and into Caanan.

I believe that all who have accepted Jesus Christ as Lord and Savior experienced a series of divine interventions just prior to, and in the early days of their walk with the Lord. God's mighty hand was first seen on their behalf freeing them from bondage to Satan, ushering them into His glorious kingdom. He them interceded in a variety of visible ways during the early days of their own personal wilderness experience to establish their faith and trust in His great love and power.

After a time, God became silent and less visible in their lives. This is essential for growth in Christ, for now the developing child must exercise his faith by studying, believing and applying God's Word to all aspects of his life. This is when he needs those memorials to renew his trust when doubt and disbelief creep in with each test and trial.

I suggest you periodically recall God's providential interventions in your life. Write them down, tell others about them and remind those who shared the experiences with you of the Lord's faithfulness. Keep them always before you. Never forget that all but two of an entire generation perished in the wilderness because they failed to trust the awesome God Who performed mighty miracles on their behalf. It is beneficial for one to frequently travel through the book of Deuteronomy.

Practical Application

My wife and I received a telephone call around 8:00 P.M. on the day after the birth of our first grandchild. We were told that our older son, a minister in the Washington D.C. area, and a few others were being held hostage by a distraught gunman. The house was surrounded by the F.B.I., SWAT team and other police agencies, preparing for the potential shootout.

We sat by the phone the next three hours wondering if our family would be reduced just one day after it expanded. We accepted that God in His sovereignty may choose to take our son home with Him that night.

My wife dealt with it by quietly dwelling on various scriptural passages and going to our bedroom to pray from time to time. But I barely moved. I spent those hours recalling how faithful God had been to me and mine, knowing He doesn't teach us to swim to let us drown. I kept those memorials before my face that entire evening. While knowing the Lord's will must be done which may require my son to leave this earth, I had total assurance that regardless of the outcome, God would not fail nor forsake us.

And of course I was not disappointed. The confrontation ended without anyone being hurt. The young man went to prison, but while there revealed evidence that the Lord entered his life when he prayed the sinner's prayer just prior to surrendering. That was a long and difficult evening, but those wonderful memorials helped me through it. And I have built one in memory of that night for future reference.

Fight The Good Fight; Finish The Race

On March 6, 1987, Eamon Coughlan, the Irish record holder at 1500 meters, was running in a qualifying heat at the World Indoor Track Championships in Indianapolis. With two and a half laps left he was tripped and fell; but got up quickly and with great effort managed to catch the leaders. With only 20 yards left in the race, he was in third place--good enough to qualify for the finals.

He looked over his shoulder to the inside, and seeing no one, he let up. But another runner, charging on the outside, passed Coughlan a yard before the finish, thus eliminating him from the finals. His great comeback effort was rendered worthless by taking his eyes off the finish line. *

Past victories, achievements and a reputation as a winner don't guarantee success in the next race, challenge or opportunity. This life is short and only a test. We will have all of eternity to celebrate and rest in God's presence and glory. In the meantime, we can't afford to let up after a fast start in which we passed a few quizzes or even a difficult mid-term exam. The course continues until the semester ends; then another begins. It's essential to remain prepared and ready until we graduate from this life and enter that which our Savior attained for us.

During the Tournament of Roses parade on New Year's Day a few years ago, a beautiful float suddenly sputtered and quit. The entire parade was held up while someone went for a can of gas. The float belonged to the Standard Oil Company. *

God's Word provides us with all we need to live the victorious life and endure to the end. His provision is more than sufficient, but must be continuously replaced as it's consumed. The Standard Oil Company has vast resources of fuel, but their truck ran out of gas at a most crucial time because someone neglected to fill its tank that day.

One of the few certainties of this life is that spiritual battles will occur. "Be self-controlled and alert. Your enemy the devil prowls around like a roaring lion looking for someone to devour" (1 Peter 5:8). Satan will choose a season to attack, and only those who feed daily on a healthy diet of God's Word will be empowered to resist him until he flees (James 4:7). We must therefore be disciplined, diligent and determined in order to finish strong.

I believe that he who prowls around like a roaring lion is tethered, and can't reach the Straight and Narrow Path upon which Jesus instructs us to travel. From there his roaring is heard and the danger of straying is evident. Following the lesson we learned early in life, however, will keep us safe – "Stay inside the lines."

A gentleman named Dean Niferatos tells of a time he was riding the Number

22 CTA bus in Chicago. It brimmed with dozing office workers, affluent shoppers and others weary from a full day of various activities. At the Clark and Webster stop, two men and a woman climbed in. The driver, a seasoned veteran immediately bellowed, "Everybody watch your valuables. There are pickpockets on board."

Women clutched their purses tightly. Men put their hands on their wallets. All eyes fixed on the trio who, looking insulted and harassed, didn't break stride as they promptly exited through the middle doors. *

Be assured that the demonic associates of the evil one are forever wanting to pick your pocket of God's blessings. Their purpose is to separate you from your Lord, cause you to lose the affection of your spouse and devotion of your children, and steal your physical health and emotional well being. They have an endless supply of enticing maneuvers, and won't let up until you depart this world. Accordingly, you can't afford to drop your guard till then.

Learn and Pursue Your Calling

Two men owned and farmed land in the same county. Each was a believer who had long experienced the goodness and faithfulness of God; and understood the division between their part and His.

One of the farmers loved the freedom and independence relative to providing for his family and serving mankind. The hard work, long periods of isolation, repetition and boredom was not a problem. Exemption from traffic jams, time clocks, personality conflicts and employing methods contrary to his preference fueled his motivation to be diligent and disciplined.

This man's duties were always properly performed, and God honored His promises as found in His Word. Consequently, this farm's production per acre was always the best within the region; and he was highly regarded within his family, church and community.

His neighbor worked hard and was honest, but the isolation, repetition and boredom depressed him. He often allowed his extensive church, social and community involvements to interfere with farming duties. As a result, his tasks were seldom, if ever, fully performed. Each harvest season brought with it worry and stress. His church friends misinterpreted these symptoms as a lack of faith in God's provision. But the farmer knew in his heart that his crop would be adequate, at best, even under optimum climatic conditions.

Prior to suffering failure and bankruptcy, this man accepted a position offered him within the state's agricultural department. He gladly exchanged loss of his occupational freedom and independence for interaction with others, a broader range of activity and reliable compensation. His extensive knowledge and experience of farms and the men who work them earned him respect within the industry. Consequently, he finally achieved success and personal fulfillment.

True followers of Christ seek their part and purpose within God's divine plan. Luke 11:9 promises those who do so will find His perfect will for their lives. The above story illustrates true contentment and fulfillment occurs when our gifts, talents, temperament and personality are blended and expressed within our endeavors. We are a diverse bunch, and thus what floats one man's boat may sink that of another.

Accept the Realities of Life

I read Dr. Scott Peck's The Road Less Travelled several years ago. It was obvious this psychologist/author had religion in his background, but no personal relationship with Christ nor extensive scriptural knowledge. That book's purpose was to share the truths of life, living and loving he discovered during years of study, contemplation and counseling.

I was fascinated to learn of the time, effort and energy expended to reach his conclusions. I had known all of these principles and concepts for years simply by reading and believing God's Word.

Scott Peck has long since made the transition from religion to Biblical Christianity. In his subsequent Further Along The Road Less Travelled, he spoke of his skepticism when he first studied the Gospels. He expected to find accounts written by disciples who tied together loose ends and embellished their biographies of Jesus. He was stunned with what they actually contained.

He said, "I was absolutely thunderstruck by the extraordinary reality of the man I found in the Gospels. I found a man who was almost continually frustrated. His frustration leaps out of virtually every page: 'What do I have to say to you? How many times do I have to say it? What do I have to do to get through to you?' I also discovered a man who was frequently sad and sometimes depressed, frequently anxious and scared. . . A man who was terribly, terribly lonely, yet often desperately needed to be alone. I discovered a man so incredibly real that no one could have made Him up.

"It occurred to me then that if the Gospel writers had been into PR and embellishment, as I had assumed, they would have created the kind of Jesus three quarters of Christians still seem to be trying to create. . . portrayed with a sweet, unending smile on His face, patting little children on the head, just strolling the earth with this unflappable, unshakable equanimity. . . But the Jesus of the Gospels – who some say is the best kept secret of Christianity – did not have much 'peace of mind,' as we ordinarily think of peace of mind in the world's terms, and insofar as we can be His followers, perhaps we won't either." [5]

Scott Peck helps me make two important points here. First, read the Bible daily and believe everything in it as the written Word of God. Instead of wasting a great allotment of time attempting to intellectually discover and comprehend the truths of this universe, you can better utilize that time applying Scripture to every aspect of your life. The validity and veracity of biblical truth will be proven over and over. The fulfillment of the many promises as you carefully perform the stated pre-condition will deepen your faith and strengthen your commitment to simply do as the Holy Spirit instructs. You will then travel a far greater distance down The Road Less Travelled by employing that method.

Secondly, accept the fact that this life has always been difficult for those attempting to live it right; and it will remain that way for as long as you are here. Ever increasing knowledge and godly wisdom will expand your abilities and human resources, but at the same time require a greater degree of responsibility and commitment. If Jesus, the only perfect person to walk the earth, struggled with frustration, depression, anxiety and loneliness, it's a certainty that each of us will also. Don't conclude that you must be on the wrong path because of the difficulties encountered; simply persevere. Just keep on keeping on, one day at a time.

I conclude this chapter with a true story proclaiming the secret of those who persevere. A woman told of her daughter Sarah who was born with a muscle missing in her foot, requiring a brace to be worn at all times. She came home from elementary school one beautiful spring day to tell her parents about competing in field day. This is when they spend the afternoon in the school yard conducting various races and other competitive events.

As the woman prepared to encourage her daughter not to let such things get her down, the little girl said, "Daddy, I won two of the races." Her mom couldn't believe it, but then Sarah said she had an advantage. "Ah, so that's it," thought Mom. "They gave her a headstart to compensate for her handicap." But the little girl went on and said, "I didn't get a headstart, Daddy. My advantage was I had to try harder."

Lesson Eight
Add Godliness to Perseverance

THIS IS NOT A REPEAT OF LESSON FOUR. Godliness and goodness sound alike and enjoy similarities, but possess distinct differences. Godliness requires a significantly higher level of character development than goodness. Peter implies we must add knowledge, self-control and perseverance to goodness to put us in position to become godly.

Bible dictionaries define goodness as strength and ability which involves moral worth; any excellence of a person or thing; power and influence. They define godliness as piety towards God, and rectitude of conduct which springs from a proper relationship with Him. It is not right actions from a sense of duty, but is that spontaneous virtue that comes from the indwelling Christ, and which reflects Him.

Goodness is a product of the soul – that one third of our total being comprised of the mind, emotions and will which are involved with the temporal. While it is right thinking and action, it is often motivated by the desire to please and impress others in order to gain a reputation as one who can be trusted and depended upon. Unlike godliness, it often promotes self-centeredness and accompanies a self-serving agenda. Goodness does not always lead to godliness, and in fact may keep us from pleasing the Lord if doing so costs us the approbation of others and the achievement of that agenda. Goodness will prompt us to do what's best for our soul, but not necessarily what's best for our spirit.

Godliness, on the other hand, is a product of the spirit – that one third of our total being that relates to God and is concerned only with the eternal. It is motivated solely by what pleases Him, and accordingly will always require goodness/virtue/character. It progressively seeks to understand the nature of God, His will (plan and purpose) for our individual life, and how to appropriate

His power which is essential for its achievement. Godliness cannot abide with self-centeredness since its focus is on what God wants; and that contends with what selfishness demands.

Has it puzzled you that certain folks within the Church who prominently exhibit goodness in difficult ways have ongoing problems within their marriage, home, finances, health, etc.? While I'm certainly not suggesting that doing good deeds and conducting ourselves in a proper way keeps us from trials and troubles, I am always concerned when immutable spiritual laws such as the sow-reap principle appear to be non-functioning.

In those instances where I have gotten to know 'good' people with never-ending trouble in the important areas of their lives, I have found what seems to be a common denominator. They pick and choose the portions of Scripture to which they willingly abide. And they give far more attention to the congregational and/or pastoral applause that makes them feel good, than they do to the still, small voice of the Holy Spirit. God often leads us in a direction that others don't understand; and asks us to do things that go unnoticed, or for which others get credit. Smorgasbord Christianity precludes us from submitting to Jesus as Lord of our life.

Chapter Eighteen What Godliness Is Not

It should be helpful at this point to understand what godliness is not. It is not dull, boring, narrow, rigid or restricted, despite popular opinion to the contrary. A God-pleasing-directed life offers much excitement and adventure while remaining within the boundaries of virtue and morality. The God of this universe is always wanting to send His child on a challenging and interesting mission, providing all that he or she will need for its successful completion.

A tell-tale sign of a person possessing goodness without godliness is, in fact, that dull, boring, narrow, rigid and restricted life alluded to above. Since reputation and the approbation of others is what fuels that person's engine, no risk of diminishing the supposedly high opinion of the doer-of-deeds will be taken. This keeps such an individual on a narrow and insipid path.

In his Come Before Winter, Pastor Charles Swindoll wrote, "We are running shy of eagles and we're running over with parrots. Content to sit safely on our evangelical perches and repeat in rapid-fire falsetto our religious words, we are fast becoming overpopulated with bright-colored birds having soft bellies, big beaks, and little heads. What would help to balance things out would be a lot more keen-eyed, wide-winged creatures willing to soar out and up, exploring the illimitable range of the kingdom of God. . . willing to return with a brief report on their findings before they leave the nest again for another fascinating adventure."

The parrots he speaks of are the many good folks who are much more concerned with impressing man than pleasing God. He says, "They like to stay in the same cage, pick over the same pan full of seeds, and listen to the same words over and over again until they can say them with ease. . . Parrots like the predicable, the secure, the strokes they get from their mutual admiration society."

The eagles he speaks of are the few godly folks who take their marching orders only from the Lord. He says, "There's not a predictable pinion in their wings! They think. They love to think. They are driven with this inner surge to search, to discover, to learn. And that means they're courageous, tough-minded, willing to ask the hard questions as they bypass the routine in vigorous pursuit of the truth. The whole truth. 'The deep things of God'. . . And unlike the intellectually impoverished parrot, eagles take risks getting their food because they hate anything that comes from a small dish of picked-over seeds. . . it's boring, dull, repetitious, and dry." [1]

The Freedom Issue

Jesus, reading from Isaiah 61:1, said, "He has sent me to proclaim freedom for the prisoners. . . to release the oppressed" (Luke 4:18). I believe He spoke of those who are literally imprisoned, those controlled by destructive addictions, those possessed or oppressed by demonic spirits, those entangled in repressive relationships and circumstances, and even those in bondage to man's way of thinking and doing.

I initially wrote this lesson around two weeks after the year 2000 presidential election. We still had no winner. While the country languished in uncertainty, the best interest of the nation was put on a distant back burner while lawyers for both sides applied intense pressure to the officials of the state that would decide this election. It was obvious that many of the tactics employed belie the continual assertions of the trailing candidate that it was all being done to assure that the will of the people is achieved.

The uncertainty, the vast philosophical differences between the candidates, and the behind-the-scenes maneuvering continually exposed by the media had Americans on both sides deeply distressed. Many Christians, unfortunately, were among those most fearful of these proceedings. They profess belief in the supremacy of God, but can't see beyond man's divisive strategy to get his own way.

Only those with true godliness seemed to be at rest. They believe that the Lord did, in fact, put in place the pillars of this world, and no one can bring them down. They are assured that even when election outcomes are contrary to their hopes, God remains in control of the affairs of man; and His will shall be done on earth as it is in heaven. They know their Lord will protect and guide them and their loved ones regardless of who is proclaimed the winner. They were therefore among the few capable of going about their daily chores free from worry, fear and anger. The uncertainty of the eventual conclusion and perceived consequences made captives of most others.

A Choice Is Required

The freedom issue is individually resolved based on answers to several questions. Who or in what do I really trust? What is the underlying basis of all decisions which ultimately affect the direction my life takes? Since I learn man's way of doing and being simply by living in this culture, what am I doing to learn God's way? Which one will I choose once I comprehend the clear distinction between the two?

In his Jesus Christ Disciple-Maker, Bill Hull provides what I believe is the only competent method for good people to become godly people. He says, "Here is the way to vital, effective fellowship: Our vertical relationship with God shapes our horizontal relationship with those around us. Fellowship with God is even more fundamental than fellowship with men. Only when we develop a humility of spirit and a willingness to submit to God will we be able to develop an open, honest kind of sharing (koinonia), giving us strength, support, and guidance for our lives. This is the holy foundation on which we must build."

Pastor Hull contends that the vitality, depth and value of our fellowship with other believers is in direct proportion to that of our personal relationship with the Lord. Our fellowship with others can have no more meaning and life than that which we have with the Father. Although they are separate and distinct relationships, that which we have with God is the foundation for all others.

He continues by saying, "Christians make a serious mistake when they seek their primary fellowship in their relationships with other Christians. Whenever we depend on other people for our spiritual vitality, we are deceiving ourselves, and in the long run we will find only frustration. Placing fellowship with others before fellowship with God creates weak, bewildered believers. Such self-limiting fellowship will tear us down, rather than builds us up."

This supports my belief in our trichotomy explained in lesson one. Our spirit and soul are separate and distinct parts of our total being. We relate to God within our spirit because He is spirit; and to others within our soul with our mind, emotions and will. It therefore follows that to be spiritually fit, we must make sufficient time daily to sit in the presence of the Lord; in prayer, Bible study and quiet contemplation. God said, "I the Lord search the heart and examine the mind, to reward a man according to his conduct, according to what his deeds deserve" (Jeremiah 17:10). Making time daily to discern what the Lord wants strengthened, corrected or altered is the way we become an "inside-out" person as mentioned earlier. We cannot, therefore, give the Lord's time to our Christian friends and expect to have a vital relationship with Him. We cannot combine those two types of fellowship since spirit and soul are not a single unit which develops under one application.

Bill Hull says it this way: "The individual Christian must develop his own walk with God. This is why personal devotions are so vital to effective Christian living. Jesus spent time with his Father in order to receive sustenance for His mission. The application, then, is for a disciple to establish communication with God on a regular basis as part of his lifestyle. Those who set aside time to communicate with God through prayer and Bible study can experience a relationship similar to the one Jesus had with His Father. What more could we want?" [2]

Chapter Nineteen The Foundation Stones of Godliness

The desire to be godly is founded on the belief that God is Who He says He is in the Bible; that He is a God of unconditional love for His creation; and a God capable of fulfilling all of His promises. That faith must then be accompanied by a willingness to trust fully in the veracity of His Word, and obey it explicitly.

The story is told of a prospector lost in the desert and dying of thirst. He stumbled towards some indiscernible object in the distance hoping to find water, but instead found a little old man sitting at a card table upon which was a display of neckties. The old gentleman responded to the prospector's request for a drink by saying, "I don't have any water, but consider buying this tie that will go well with your torn and tattered outfit."

Despite the straggler's abrasive response to his sales pitch, the little old man directs him to a nice restaurant with a plentiful water supply. "It is just four miles from here, over that mound and due north across the hot sand," he replied.

Several hours later, the prospector was seen crawling towards the little old man sitting at his card table. The tie salesman inquired as to whether or not his directions led him to the restaurant. The half-dead prospector gasped, "I found it, but they wouldn't let me in without a tie."

A loving God will meet my every need without feeding my frustrations. But I must believe that He is unlike many people who will help me only if it serves their own ends.

The next step or foundation stone is my awareness of God's eternal plan and purpose for my life. The specific details are not required at this point, just the assurance that such a plan and purpose exist. I must add to that the belief that the Lord will make His plan known as needed, and intervene and intercede on my behalf as I attempt to follow His lead.

A medical student doing a rotation in toxicology at the poison control center spoke of a frantic call from a woman who caught her daughter eating ants. The intern calmed the woman by assuring her that the ants would do the child no harm. At the end of the conversation, however, the young mother mentioned that she gave her daughter some ant poison to eat to kill the bugs. At that point the medical student instructed the woman to bring the little girl to the emergency room immediately.

Believing, trusting and submitting to God's guidance does not permit me to take leave of my senses. I must, in fact, be most diligent in acquiring ongoing relevant knowledge and making full use of the resources and faculties the Lord provided.

The final step or foundation stone to the godliness process is the lifelong dedication to resisting the human tendency to take back control and pursue my own agenda. We Christians are most adept at convincing ourselves and others that what we want is God's revealed will.

A father received a note from his son away at college. It read, "Dear Dad, $chool i$ really great. I am making lot$ of friend$ and $tudying very hard. I

$imply can't think of anything I need at the moment, $o if you would like, ju$t $end me a card of encouragement, a$ I would love to hear from you. Love, Your $on"

The father replied, "I kNOw that astroNOmy, ecoNOmics and oceaNOgraphy are eNOugh to keep even a hoNOr student like you busy. Do NOt forget that the pursuit of kNOwledge is a NOble task, and you can never study eNOugh. Love, Dad"

We may convince ourselves and others that our wishes are God's desires for our life, but our heavenly Father is not fooled. The need to be open, honest and transparent at all times saves energy and protects us from frustration and disillusionment.

Discard Your Logic of What is Fair, Just, Reasonable & Effective

Godliness requires me to know and do things God's way. Because of the vast discrepancies between His methods and man's schemes, I must believe Isaiah 55:8,9. This passage says, "'For my thoughts are not your thoughts, neither are your ways my ways,' declares the Lord. 'As the heavens are higher than the earth, so are my ways higher than your ways, and my thoughts than your thoughts.'"

Without accepting the truth of that statement on blind faith, my intellect won't permit me to apply much of what's in Scripture. Until I submit to godly wisdom, I'm not capable of leaving the low road of human reasoning. Let's look at a few of the parables Jesus used to demonstrate what I mean.

Lavish Love

Luke 15:11-32 tells us about the prodigal father who models the love of God for the lost. I realize the adjective prodigal is generally applied to the wayward son.

That is justifiable since one use of that word means "wasteful in a reckless way." A second definition, however, is "very plentiful; generous or lavish."

With both meanings in mind, let's see if we agree with the Lord Who sets the father's actions as a standard for us to follow. Let's say you honored your son's request for one half of your existing estate to be used for some type of European venture. Then you didn't hear from him for several years. Suddenly he shows up at your door – broke, homeless and seeking a janitorial position with your company. What would be your response?

Would you be so happy that he was alive and in good health that you welcome him home with open arms? Knowing he squandered one half of that for which you worked tirelessly over a period of many years, would you throw a lavish party celebrating his return? Would you immediately restore to him his former place in your home and heart? Would you risk offending your other son who has been faithful and obedient to you throughout his life? Think about your answers to those questions, then compare them with the facts of that parable.

Compassion For the Lost

Let's look at Luke 15:4-7 where Jesus implies that no wise shepherd would think twice about leaving ninety-nine of his sheep unguarded in a wilderness pasture to look for one that strayed. And when he finds it, he carries it back and throws a party. In the same passage, the Lord tells us that there is more rejoicing in heaven over one sinner who repents than ninety-nine good people who do not sin.

If you belonged to a one hundred member church, how would you feel about your pastor cancelling one or more Sunday services to look for the husband who walked out on his wife and children? If he found him and helped him work through his problems and be reunited with his family, would you attend the party thrown by the pastor to celebrate the man's return? And if you have always played by the rules with no conscious need for repentance, how do you feel about God being happier about one who has sown wild oats and then repented and returned to Him, than He is about you and ninety-eight of your straight-laced fellow Christians who never strayed?

Dealing With Rebellion

Jesus tells us through the parable found in Matthew 13:24-30 to allow the weeds to grow with the grain so as not to risk uprooting any part of the crop. Wait until the grain is fully grown and clearly discernible from the weeds, then separate them and destroy the weeds.

Apply that concept to a charitable or ministry organization you direct; established to achieve a certain purpose over a specified period of time. While all the members of such initially appeared to be in agreement with your leadership objectives and methods, a few boldly voiced opposition to your philosophy and directives as time went on.

Do you wait until the work is completed before casting out the dissenters as Jesus instructs, or do you quickly show them who's boss and the door? Are you willing to endure their criticism to avoid a disruption to the progress achieved towards the group's purpose? Is it possible you haven't done things exactly as you said you would, and thus you should at least entertain their complaints to see if they contain any validity? Do you persevere to avoid the rebels taking with them one or more who may be misled, or do you cast them out with their first act of defiance and let the chips fall where they may? Do you do it God's way or man's way?

Accumulation of Wealth

Let's look at Luke 12:16-25. Jesus denounces the man who builds storehouses for his great accumulation of crops and goods to provide for a lengthy and prosperous retirement. In fact, He calls him a fool.

Doesn't that fly in the face of conventional wisdom? TV commercials of various financial service firms proclaim that fools are those who don't accumulate as much as possible for their post employment life. Isn't the person who achieves great success and prudently manages his/her finances in preparation for their later years to be envied and emulated? Does it make sense to give freely from the produce of your labor to those in need; possibly requiring you to continue working beyond retirement age? Don't you owe it to yourself to have a period of leisure, luxury and travel since you worked so hard for so long? Can you dare trust the Lord to give you the health and enthusiasm to continue earning your keep and living out your days without needing expensive assistance?

As you can see from the above examples of the Lord's radical teachings that being godly – doing thing His way – is far more difficult than just being good. You must know and understand how to apply God's instructions to your day-to-day life. You must dare to believe His methods will work as He says despite their contradiction to human reasoning. You must choose to trust the Lord, desiring to obey and please Him even if it costs you to do so.

Chapter Twenty It Gets Easier

Our Creator has established immutable spiritual laws comparable to those of nature which maintain order within this physical universe. One of the few things I've retained from my high school chemistry class is that water is comprised of two parts hydrogen and one part oxygen. Nothing more, nothing less, and nothing different will produce that particular life sustaining element.

The abundant life Jesus came to provide for us requires knowledge and application of the spiritual laws. Just as a chemist, physicist or inventor must know and submit to the laws governing their particular discipline, those who desire to be godly must do likewise. And since the spiritual laws found in the Gospels are immutable – never changing – they work just as the Bible says they will each and every time they are correctly and completely applied. Each success promotes greater confidence and comprehension, thus it becomes easier and more natural to live in harmony within God's plan and purpose.

The principal spiritual laws appear to be Reciprocity, Use, Perseverance, Responsibility, Greatness, Unity and Harmony, and Miracles. A brief explanation of each follows; but for a detailed study of these laws, read Pat Robertson's Secret Kingdom. [3]

Law of Reciprocity

Jesus best expresses this law in Luke 6:38 when He says, "Give, and it will be given to you. A good measure, pressed down, shaken together and running over, will be poured into your lap. For with the measure you use, it will be measured to you." A loose paraphrase says, "Be concerned with sending a fully loaded ship out, rather than standing on the dock waiting for your's to come in. If you do, it will."

The old farm lift or reciprocating pump illustrates this spiritual law. Pumping the handle drives the piston up and down inside the pump cylinder which forces out the air, leaves a temporary vacuum and then fills it with water. Upper and lower flap valves control what goes into and comes out of the cylinder. They contain leather parts which soften and create an airtight seal only when wet. This occurs when the user pours in a container of water and primes the pump, which then provides a steady stream of cool, fresh water from the underground spring or well as long as the handle is pumped. Prior to modern plumbing performing this process for us, you had to give the little you had in hopes of getting more and better in return.

The law of reciprocity involves the giving of our time, energy, talents, money and other resources. Our part is to give and keep giving; God's part is to measure and provide what and when He wills for us to receive in return. As Solomon said, "Sow your seed in the morning, and at evening let not your hands be idle, for you do not know which will succeed, whether this or that, or whether both will do equally well" (Ecclesiastes 11:6).

Law of Use

The Lord teaches us this law through His Parable of the Talents. The master spoke to the servants who made full use of that which was given them saying,

"Well done, good and faithful servant! You have been faithful with a few things; I will put you in charge of many things. Come and share your master's happiness" (Matthew 25:21). Jesus reiterated this spiritual principle later in that passage when He said, "For everyone who has will be given more, and he will have an abundance. Whoever does not have, even what he has will be taken from him" (Matthew 25:29).

God created each of us for a specific task and purpose. All who are called to serve Him are expected to diligently use all that He provides in our own unique way for the expansion of the Lord's kingdom. I read somewhere that evangelist Dwight L. Moody was confronted by a critical brother who questioned his style of pulpit evangelism. Moody's response was, "How many people have you led to Christ lately?" The critical brother lowered his head, obviously embarrassed. Moody then said, "I like my method better than yours."

Pastor Chuck Swindoll, in his Living On The Ragged Edge, says it this way. "You have been set on this earth as a unique jewel, as a gem that has certain sparkling possibilities when the light of the Son hits them. As you glisten and gleam, you encourage, enlighten, and strengthen those who are lost in the gloom of their personal swamp. Even though you may feel insignificant and not that gifted, God can and wants to use you." [4]

Law of Perseverance

Jesus told us to never give up or give in so long as we were trusting God to act on our behalf within His will as expressed in the Bible. The Lord said, "Ask and it will be given to you; seek and you will find; knock and the door will be opened to you. For everyone who asks receives; he who seeks finds; and to him who knocks, the door will be opened" (Matthew 7:7,8). The implication is that you will receive, find, or see the door open if you refuse to quit asking, seeking or knocking until it happens.

Human nature takes a far more negative view of things. It says, "If it wasn't for bad luck, I would have no luck at all. So why even try since I can't win for losing no matter what I do." This attitude echoes the story of the man on the streets of Belfast one night. A dark figure suddenly emerged from the shadows, grabbed him around the neck and stuck the point of a knife against his throat. The assailant then asked in a gruff voice, "Catholic or Protestant?" Seized with panic, the man saw that he had only a 50-50 chance of survival should he answer that question. Thinking he found a way out he said, "I'm a Jew!" The attacker sneered in response, "Aha! I'm the luckiest Arab terrorist in Belfast!"

In contrast, the Bible makes it clear it is always too soon to quit if we are trusting God for that healing or loved one's salvation; if we are looking for the Lord's specific guidance or blessing on our efforts; if we are seeking the opportunity to serve Him in a significant manner; or if we are waiting for God's performance of a scriptural promise when the condition has been met. Isaiah says, "But those who hope in the Lord will renew their strength. They will soar on wings like eagles; they will run and not grow weary, they will walk and not be faint" (Isaiah 40:31).

Most who accomplished great things in life such as Abraham Lincoln, Thomas Edison, Henry Ford and Winston Churchill, literally failed their way to success. The distinguished heavyweight boxer James Corbett once said, "To be champion, fight one more round." Lesson seven expounds on this important spiritual law.

Law of Responsibility

Jesus said, "From everyone who has been given much, much will be demanded; and from the one who has been entrusted with much, much more will be asked" (Luke 12:48). The manner in which we conduct ourselves as parents, teachers, managers, employers, ministers and government officials has a substantial effect on those subordinate to us. The greater our realm of authority or influence, the more rigid is God's standard of responsibility. We must take this matter seriously.

Responsibility has everything to do with character. Dwight L. Moody once said, "Character is what you are in the dark." This requires the recognition that all I am and have is of the Lord, and He demands total honesty and much diligence in the performance of all my duties. Pastor Bill Hybels, in his Honest To God?, uses the word authentic to describe Christians who honor and obey God in every area and aspect of their lives. He says, "Authenticity means consistency – between words and actions, and between claimed values and actual priorities." Later on he informs the reader that the Lord expects us to maintain this responsible life style over the long haul. His final chapter reminds those desiring Christian authenticity of their need to draw closer to God on a daily basis, and progressively improve in every area of their life. Three safeguards recommended for maintaining these practices and finishing well are discipline, accountability and proper pacing. [5]

The seriousness of this law is reiterated by the Lord's brother. He says, "NOT MANY of you should presume to be teachers, my brothers, because you know that we who teach will be judged more strictly" (James 3:1). Most positions of authority or influence involve some form of teaching. So keep the Lord's judgment in mind as you dispense instruction, and be sure to do so in a responsible fashion.

Law of Greatness

Jesus tells us that the leader in God's kingdom is the one who serves. He says in Matthew 18:4, "Therefore, whoever humbles himself like this child is the greatest in the kingdom of God." And He says in Matthew 23:12, "for whoever exalts himself will be humbled, and whoever humbles himself will be exalted." The greatest gunslinger in the old, wild west was he with the most notches on his belt – each signifying one who no longer lives. The greatest disciple of Christ, on the other hand, is he who refuses to subdue another, helping them instead to live life more fully.

Truly great people are those who honor their word even when it's to their detriment. They seek ongoing improvement to their character, further knowledge of God, and progressive Christian maturity rather than fame or fortune. They take risks and allow themselves to be vulnerable for the benefit of others. They are honest, faithful and dependable; unconcerned with popularity and forever willing to stand up for the truth. They are the first to leave the crowd when it's headed in the wrong direction, and the last to compromise their walk with the Lord.

I love the story told of an old man walking the beach at dawn who saw a young man throwing starfish back in the sea. In response to the elder's question as to what he was doing, the younger responded that the stranded starfish would die if left there until the sun arose. "But the beach goes on for many miles, and you can only cover a short distance before that occurs. So what difference can you make?," asked the old gentleman. The young man looked at the starfish in his hand, then tossed it to safety in the waves. "It makes a big difference to that one," he said. *

Great people have no interest in the applause of the crowd. They don't save their exploits until an audience has gathered. They try instead to save from the fires of hell all whom God brings to them.

The Law of Unity and Harmony

Jesus teaches in Matthew 18:19, "Again, I tell you that if two of you on earth agree about anything you ask for, it will be done for you by my Father in heaven." In Matthew 12:25 He says, "Every kingdom divided against itself will be ruined, and every city or household divided against itself will not stand." And while in prayer to the Father for all present and future believers He said, "May they be brought to complete unity to let the world know that you sent me and have loved them even as you have loved me" (John 17:23).

It's clear that the above passages do not limit God's command and commission to just those within our own family, congregation, denomination, ethnic group or race. They require us instead to pull down all walls of division, and love and disciple all men everywhere. Bill McCartney, founder of the Promise Keepers Ministry, says at their rallies, "But what I know is Almighty God wants to bring all men together regardless of their ethnic origin, denominational background, or style of worship. There's only one criterion for this kind of unity: to love Jesus and be born of the Spirit of God. Can we look one another in the eye – black, white, red, brown, yellow, Baptist, Presbyterian, Assemblies of God, Catholic, and so on – and get together on this common ground: 'We believe in Salvation through Christ alone, and we have made Him Lord of our lives?' Is that not the central, unifying reality of our existence? And if it is, can we not focus on that and call each other brother instead of always emphasizing our differences?"

Speaking of brothers, once upon a time two of them lived on adjoining farms. They worked side by side in peace and harmony for many years, sharing machinery and trading labor and goods as needed. But one day all that came to an end when a minor misunderstanding grew into a major difference, then exploded into an exchange of bitter words followed by weeks of silence.

About that time a carpenter carrying his tool box knocked on the older brother's door. He asked if he needed some jobs done, saying he was looking for a few days work. The farmer replied that he would like an eight foot fence built between his house and the one next to him. "See that creek on the edge of my property?" he asked. "It used to be a meadow, but my neighbor, who is also my younger brother, bulldozed the river levee and created a stream between us. He is so deceitful that I never want him on my property again."

The carpenter said he understood, and the older brother provided him with all the lumber, nails and equipment needed. He then left for the day to shop for supplies in the nearest town. When he returned at sunset, the carpenter was putting the finishing touches on his project. The older brother was ready to erupt in anger when he saw that the man had built a beautiful bridge over the creek rather than a fence as he had been instructed.

Just then he saw his younger brother come across the bridge with his hand extended. He apologized for his words and actions, and thanked him for being much bigger than he, and willing to forgive and make amends. As they stood and talked with one another, the older brother saw the carpenter walk away with his tools on his shoulder.

He called out to him, asking him to stay a few more days and do some other projects. "I can give you much more work," said the older brother in appreciation for what the man had done. "I would love to stay," replied the carpenter, "but I have many more bridges to build."

Law of Miracles

Jesus expressed His desire that the miraculous work which He performed while upon this earth would be continued by His followers. He said, "I tell you the

176

truth, anyone who has faith in me will do what I have been doing. He will do even greater things than these, because I am going to the father. And I will do whatever you ask in my name, so that the Son may bring glory to the Father" (John 14:12-13).

The doctrine of Cessationism which disputes this passage, began with the reformers somewhere around the fifteenth century, and has been accepted and carried on by many Protestant theologians since then. A professor at Princeton Seminary, Benjamin Breckinridge Warfield, popularized this belief through his book written in 1918 entitled Counterfeit Miracles. He wrote, "It is very clear from the record of the New testament that the extraordinary charismata (gift of miracles) were not (after the very first days of the Church) the possession of all Christians, but supernatural gifts to the few.

"These gifts were not the possession of the primitive Christian as such; nor for that matter of the Apostolic Church or the Apostolic age for themselves; they were distinctly for the authentication of the Apostles. They were part of the credentials of the Apostles as the authoritative agents of God in founding the Church. Their function thus confined them to distinctly the Apostolic Church, and they necessarily passed away with it." (6)

A current pastor and former Dallas Theological Seminary professor, Dr. Jack Deere, subscribed to and taught this doctrine for many years to those preparing for full-time ministry. But then, through a series of divinely orchestrated events over an extended period of time, the Spirit of God sovereignly took him by surprise. He became associated with a few men of God through whom the Lord performed healing and other miracles in Dr. Deere's presence. He then took a fresh look at the Scriptures and discovered that his cherished arguments against miraculous gifts were based on prejudice and a lack of personal experience rather than on the Bible.

Dr. Deere extensively researched all that the Word of God had to say about miracles. His new knowledge and understanding led him to forsake the Cessationist argument, costing him his teaching position at Dallas Seminary. The Lord has since opened his mind and heart to the continued existence of the gifts of the Holy Spirit, and led him to write an exceptional book entitled Surprised By The Power Of The Spirit. [7]

Chapter Twenty One See Things Through God s Eyes

A change in perspective is required to achieve godliness. Man and God have a very different value system. Good people lacking godliness focus on what they think is best for themselves and others. When reaching out to those in need, they give or help them acquire what they themselves have or would want in similar circumstances. They're influenced by what secular forces around and about them define as good, necessary or blessings.

Godly people, on the other hand, are concerned only with what pleases God or what draws themselves or others closer to Him. They study Scripture to comprehend the Lord's way of thinking and doing. They want to know what is the will of God for themselves and for those to whom they minister, in each and every situation.

Paul said it this way in Romans 8:5-8: "Those who live according to the sinful nature have their minds set on what that nature desires; but those who live in accordance with the Spirit have their mind set on what the Spirit desires. The mind of sinful man is death, but the mind controlled by the Spirit is life and peace; the sinful mind is hostile to God. It does not submit to God's law, nor can it do so.

Those controlled by the sinful nature cannot please God."

The following anecdote conveys my point in a manner superior to further explanation: A very wealthy man once took his son on a trip to the country to help him understand how fortunate he was to live in such prosperity. They spent a couple of days and nights with a poor farmer and his family.

On the return trip home, the father asked the son how he enjoyed the trip, and if he now understands how poor people can be. The young boy responded that he had a great time, then elucidated what he had learned.

He said, "I saw that we have one dog but they have four. We have a pool that reaches to the middle of our garden while they have a creek that never ends. We have imported lanterns in our garden, but they have the moon and stars to light their fields at night. Our patio extends to the front yard while their front door opens to what seems like the whole world. We live on what I thought was a big piece of land, but their fields go further than my eyes could see. We have servants to serve us, while they serve others. We buy our food, but they grow theirs. We have walls around our property to protect us, while they have friends and caring neighbors to protect them." Since the father was speechless, his son added, "Thanks Dad for showing me how poor we are."

I would allow that the difference between the perspective of these two members of one family is comparable to that of man and God. Therefore human reasoning will never produce godliness. It must be discovered in the Book and earnestly applied to our lives.

The Real Challenge

Becoming ever-more godly requires a persistent and gallant effort. But the real challenge is to balance our godliness with our humanity. While on this earth, Jesus refused to sin yet never stopped ministering to sinners. He expects no less from us.

Those who are rigid, demanding, harsh and unforgiving with themselves, are generally likewise or more so with others. As society becomes increasingly decadent, we will continue to see and hear in public that which was seen and heard only in private not long ago. While our spirit may be indignant, saddened and disturbed, the sensual aspect of our being may be aroused and interested. Although it's essential that our spirit rule our will and forbid us yielding to temptation, it's equally important to prohibit guilt from rendering its unjust verdict on our humanity. Only then can we exhibit and distribute God's grace to others.

Don't become so heavenly minded that you're no earthly good. And don't get so square that you can't understand and minister to round people.

Lesson Nine
Add Brotherly Kindness to Godliness

Brotherly kindness, while contrary to man's self-centered nature, is the evidence of attaining a high level of practical Christianity. Peter implies that a strong faith in God and His Word, moral excellence (goodness), scriptural knowledge, self-control in all aspects of life, ability to persevere, and godliness are prerequisites for consistently caring for one another. Paul said, "Be devoted to one another in brotherly love. Honor one another above yourselves" (Romans 12:10).

Peter's second letter to the believers from which the above progression is taken, was concerned with problems within the Church. He wrote primarily to warn about the false teachers that had infiltrated Christ's disciples. They were sensuous, arrogant, greedy, covetous, and peddled damaging doctrine. The apostle urged those who belonged to the Lord to keep a close watch on their personal life, and then look out for one another. He wanted them to protect each other from Satan's schemes to draw them away from the teachings of Jesus.

Brotherly kindness, like the other traits, attitudes and responsibilities covered thus far in this book, is not narrow nor restricted. Our God is a big God, and His purpose for each of us called by His name is likewise grand. That which He commands us to do is thus far wider and deeper than that perceived by natural tendencies. With that in mind, I wish to suggest a dozen ways in which each of us can express brotherly kindness to others. With a little effort, I'm sure you can add quite a few more.

Chapter Twenty   Two Helping Those Incapable of Helping Themselves

God said through His prophet Isaiah, "Is not this the kind of fasting I have chosen: to loose the chains of injustice and untie the cords of the yoke, to set the oppressed free and break every yoke? Is it not to share your food with the hungry and to provide the poor wanderer with shelter--when you see the naked to clothe him, and not to turn away from your own flesh and blood?" (Isaiah 58:6,7).

Reaching out to the helpless, hopeless and poor is certainly expected of us by the Lord. Sometimes we are to directly involve ourselves with the unfortunate. Other times we may be called to be a part of a ministry or charitable organization that helps those in need. And still other times the Lord would have us contribute financially to such groups; or perhaps all three at the same time.

Of course, God compensates us well when we serve others as He directs. Continuing on with the above passage, Isaiah says, "then your light will break forth like the dawn, and your healing will quickly appear; then your righteousness will go before you and the glory of the Lord will be your rear guard. Then you will call, and the Lord will answer; you will cry for help, and he will say: Here am I. If you do away with the yoke of oppression, with the pointing finger and malicious talk, and if you spend yourselves in behalf of the hungry and satisfy the needs of the oppressed, then your light will rise in the darkness, and your night will become like the noonday. The Lord will guide you always; he will satisfy your needs in a sun-scorched land and will strengthen your frame. You will be like a well-watered garden, like a spring whose waters never fail" (Isaiah 58:8-11).

It would seem from the above passage that the best way to be healed or delivered from darkness and depression, set free from circumstances that bind and oppress, and receive quick answers to prayers is to be involved in helping those incapable of helping themselves. If we desire to be guided by the Lord at all times, have our needs met and be vibrant and strong, we must sincerely minister God's truth and love to those in dire straits that He brings to us.

Refusing to Help Those Who Won't Help Themselves

This is where religion and Biblical Christianity collide head on. We must comprehend the stark difference between discipling and enabling despite their similar appearance. We learn from the Isaiah 58:8-11 passage that all who are able much reach out to those less fortunate then themselves if they desire God's blessings on their own lives.

We all know those who insist on others doing for them what they are capable of doing for themselves. These same folks claim they could not possibly help another because of their own sad state of affairs.

To these we need to be kind and patient, seeking God's discernment as to how to help them. We should teach them the Word, and encourage them to live in accordance with it. And by God's grace we may uncover the source that hinders or disables them, opening their eyes to what has them bound. Speaking the truth in love is vital here.

We must not, however, be willing to bear the consequences of their poor choices, or do for them what they can do for themselves. This enables them to remain as they are. It's often the easy way and the path of least resistance; perhaps even achieving for ourselves a sense of worth or popularity. But it's contrary to teaching and exhorting them to become true disciples of Christ, and that must always be our goal.

Providing Opportunities to Those Seeking a Chance to be Productive

The exhausted adage that "God helps those who help themselves" is not scripturally correct. The Bible reveals that the Lord remains available to those who recognize their own helplessness and total dependance on Him. As we see in the Isaiah 58:9 passage, "Then you will call and the Lord will answer; you will cry for help, and He will say: Here am I."

Providing opportunities for disadvantaged people to provide for themselves by using their God-given gifts and talents is not in accordance with that false statement. The purpose here is to open doors and give encouragement to those who are involuntarily dependant on others. Give them what God has freely given you, a chance to fulfill their hopes and dreams. It's within that opportunity that they may feel inadequate and overwhelmed; hopefully leading them to seek God's presence, help and guidance.

In his Honest To God?, Pastor Bill Hybels lists providing opportunities that offer stimulation, achievement and fulfillment as one of the seven most common languages of love. [1]. Providing ways for others to gain self respect, confidence and a chance to become that for which God has created and called them is certainly an act of brotherly kindness.

It doesn't have to be anything grand or significant. Sometimes a word of encouragement at the proper time, a nudge in the right direction, or a chance for recognition of some accomplishment is all it takes. "Rags to Riches" stories often speak of a teacher, coach or older neighbor who guided, encouraged or challenged the one who succeeded. Their efforts had an exponential benefit on the recipient which far exceeded that which was given.

In his Bringing Out The Best In People, psychologist and author Dr. Alan Loy McGinnis provides twelve rules for achieving the book's title. [2] A few of them are as follows:

Expect the best from people you lead.

Create an environment where failure is not fatal.

If they are going anywhere near where you want to go, climb on other people's bandwagon.

Tell stories of those who overcame.

Recognize and applaud achievement.

Sincerely wanting God's best for others, and doing whatever you can to help them receive it, is a true expression of Paul's admonition to be devoted to one another in brotherly love.

Chapter Twenty   Three Caring for Your Own Flesh and Blood

The Lord commands us in various areas of the Bible to help, provide for and take care of those placed in our trust. This would include our spouse, children, grandchildren, parents, grandparents, siblings, and any other blood relative who's in need with no one to help.

In his address to the 1991 Wheaton College graduating class, Pastor Charles Swindoll spoke of "What I wish they had told me when I graduated." One of his five topics was entitled "Home." Pastor Swindoll said, "I wished they would have told me when I graduated, that my most significant work, my lasting legacy in life, would not take place in the pulpit before the public, but behind closed doors, with my wife, our children, and our grandchildren. . .

"I have learned that many in ministry prefer their study, travel, or public ministry at the church. Why? In all candor you get stroked there. Furthermore, if I may be painfully honest, it's easier to fake it there. But the unvarnished truth emerges at home. It's much more exacting, demanding, yet I must add, rewarding." [3]

Individuals who succeed in ministry, business, sports or other endeavors often lose their family along the way. That's an awful price to pay for success. And even if thousands come to know the Lord through your ministry involvement, God is grieved if it's done at the expense of your family.

Speaker and author Steve Farrar devoted a substantial portion of a particular chapter in his Finishing Strong to this topic. Prior to being married and having children, a friend asked him what was his greatest fear about going into ministry. He responded, "Being successful in ministry and losing my family." It was a major concern of his even at that early stage in life because every pastor he had known, but one, watched his children trash their faith and trust in God when they became adults.

How can we expect those dependant upon us to love the God we serve if we do so to their detriment? The hypocrisy of that causes them to hate the Lord we profess to love. The old saying, "What you do is so loud I can't hear what you say," is relevant here.

Steve Farrar speaks of the famous British missionary of many years past, C. T. Studd, who served tirelessly in China. He then returned home for several years, but felt called to go to Africa. He did so and didn't see his wife again for seventeen years. How does that line up with the Lord's claim that "the two of them became one" when they were joined in marriage? Can a man love, care for and cherish his wife as the Bible commands while they are continents apart for seventeen years?

He spoke also of three unidentified ministers who made a great impact for Christ during the early days of the twentieth century. One spent an average of ten months per year for fifteen years away from home. As a result, his oldest daughter committed suicide and his wife divorced him. Another traveled extensively throughout the untied States while his children were growing up. One son became a public figure who declared his homosexuality and rejected Christianity. And the third was a gifted evangelist who traveled for many years with his wife who organized his city-wide meetings across America. He regretted during his later years that his sons, raised by a nanny while their parents shared the Gospel, would have nothing to do with the God of Whom he preached. (4)

Use Positions of Authority for the Benefit of Others

Calling many who are in political positions of power and privilege public servants is a misnomer of epic proportions. But is shouldn't be. Paul said, "EVERYONE MUST submit himself to the governing authorities, for there is no authority except that which God has established. The authorities that exist have been established by God" (Romans 13:11). If that be true, as I believe it is because of its source, all governing authorities have a serious responsibility to serve and protect their citizens. Each person holding a political office should use that position to bring about necessary changes in laws, rules and attitudes towards the disadvantaged, weak, persecuted and forgotten.

History allegedly records that eleventh century King Henry III of Bavaria grew wary of the pressures and expectations of life as a monarch. He applied to Prior Richard of a local monastery, seeking acceptance as a contemplative who would spend the remainder of his life there in prayer and quiet service.

Prior Richard reminded King Henry that a pledge of obedience is required at the monastery. "That will be most difficult for you since you have been a king," he said. But Henry responded, "I understand. The rest of my life I will be obedient to you, as Christ leads you."

"Then I will tell you what to do," said Prior Richard. "Go back to your throne and serve faithfully in the place where God has put you."*

Government officials, parents, ministry leaders, employers and teachers all have tremendous opportunities to help, encourage and strengthen those that God has placed in their care. And while it's a privilege and responsibility to do so, it is also an act of brotherly kindness.

Ask Questions, Then Listen Intently to the Answers

James said, "My dear brothers, take note of this: Everyone should be quick to listen, slow to speak and slow to become angry" (James 1:19). Most preachers using this passage like to point out that since God gave us two ears but only one mouth, He obviously intended us to listen twice as much as we speak.

Unfortunately, that's not the way it is for most of us. If those faculties functioned like our joints, most of our tongues would wear out long before our ears. But it's truly an act of brotherly kindness to care enough to listen to those with real burdens, heartaches and difficult circumstances.

A prospector had been lost in the desert for two weeks. Dying of hunger, thirst and exhaustion, he crawled up to the door of a mission outpost. After eating, drinking and resting, he asked to borrow the missionary's horse to go to the nearest town for supplies.

The man of God granted his request, gave him directions, but told him the horse will only move when you say "Thank God;" then stop only when you say "Amen." Not paying much attention, the man mounted the animal and said "giddyup," but it didn't move. The missionary repeated his instructions, the prospector said "Thank God," and the horse began walking.

He soon learned that the more he said "Thank God," the faster the horse went. Getting it up to a full gallop he suddenly saw a cliff rapidly approaching. He yelled, "Whoa boy! Stop! Halt!," but the horse maintained his stride. Fortunately he remembered just in time what the missionary said, and screamed "Amen!," The steed stopped inches from the edge of the cliff.

Greatly relieved with his heart still racing, the prospector sat back in the saddle, wiped his brow, took a deep breath and said, "Thank God!"

I suspect things went downhill from there. So just as it's best for our own well-being to listen carefully, it can be beneficial to others. The best thing we can do for the hurting folks the Lord brings our way, is often just to help them clarify in their own minds what is lacking in their lives, and what may be the root cause of their unhappiness.

Asking pertinent questions, listening intently to their answers, then requesting further clarification may enable them to see for the first time the source of their problems. Asking such things as "Where do you want to go in life?," "What would you like to change?," and "What behavior patterns do you wish to alter?" helps them probe their innermost needs, desires and hopes. By so doing, we can gently convey that they are primarily responsible for making the necessary changes in their life. And if they reveal proper thinking and intentions, we can then encourage them to proceed.

Introduce the God of Love and Power to Those Lost Without Him

This, of course, is the ultimate act of brotherly kindness. I chose to place it in the middle rather than at the beginning since it's the core reason and purpose for reaching out to our fellow wanderers on this earth.

An eastern newspaper reported the following story some years ago. A woman was driving home one evening and noticed a large truck behind her staying uncomfortably close. As she sped up to create safe space between them, it did likewise and remained close to her rear bumper.

Now frightened, she exited the expressway; but the truck driver did likewise.

She turned onto a main road hoping to lose him in traffic, but he ran a red light and continued the chase. Nearing the panic point, she swerved into a gas station, jumped out of the car and screamed for help.

The truck pulled in behind her and its driver also exited the vehicle quickly. He ran to the woman's car, jerked open the back door and pulled out the man hiding in the back seat whom he could see from his high vantage point.*

Much like the scared woman, those who most need God's love, mercy and protection often run from the only One Who can save them. Believing the Lord is angry and only wants to punish them, the last thing they want to do is turn to Him.

There is no greater act of brotherly kindness we can do for anyone than leading them to the God of the Bible. Teaching them about the Jesus found in the Gospels will, in time, help them dispel their false notions of Him. And displaying for them sincere concern, patience and understanding will promote their comprehension and stimulate their desire for communion with the Lord.

Raising God-Fearing Difference Makers

We have an impact on generations to come and the countless people their lives touch when we raise our children in accordance with biblical principles; and lead them to their own saving knowledge of Jesus Christ. Moses said to the Israelites, "What other nation is so great as to have their gods near them the way the Lord our God is near us whenever we pray to him? And what other nation is so great as to have righteous decrees and laws as this body of laws I am setting before you today? Only be careful, and watch yourselves closely so that you do not forget the things your eyes have seen or let them slip from your heart as long as you live. Teach them to your children and their children after them" (Deuteronomy 4: 7-9).

A farmer was teaching his young son to plow. He stressed the need to maintain straight lines, telling him to fix his eyes on a distant object and continuously move towards it. Then he left to perform his numerous chores.

He returned two hours later to see plow lines that wavered about. Upset with his son, he asked the lad why he had not obeyed his instructions. The son, however, insisted he did as he was told. "What did you focus on?," asked the distraught father. "A cow," replied the boy.

Teaching our children and grandchildren the absolutes of God's Word will provide for them the essential unchanging and unmoving object for their focus. Only in this way can they progressively travel the "Straight and Narrow" path which pleases the Lord, and become productive citizens and disciples of Christ.

Chapter Twenty Four Refuse to Gossip and Spread Unkind Rumors of Others

Table salt is comprised of two chemicals--sodium and chlorine. Sodium achieves nothing on its own, and must be linked with another element to be productive. Chlorine, on the other hand, is a poisonous gas with an offensive odor. Yet joined together they preserve meat and bring out the taste in many foods.

Love and truth function much the same way. Love not founded on truth has little value, and in fact seldom qualifies as real love. Truth not spoken in love, on the other hand, is poisonous and offensive. The Gospel message is properly presented, illustrated and applied only when truth and love abide in unity and harmony. *

Leviticus 19:16 says, "Do not go around spreading slander among your people." Proverbs 11:13 says, "A gossip betrays a confidence, but a trustworthy man keeps a secret." Proverbs 10:18 says, "He who conceals hatred has lying lips, and he who utters slander is a fool." Proverbs 26:20 says, "Without wood, a fire goes out; without gossip a quarrel dies down." And Paul instructed his disciples Timothy and Titus to admonish the wives of deacons and older women in the church to be reverent in their speech and refuse to talk maliciously.

It is thus an act of brotherly kindness to refuse to spread any rumor until it is confirmed as truth. It should then be repeated only if it will be a help and blessing to both the one it concerns and the one to whom it is spoken.

Forgiving Others of Mistakes, Insults and Offenses

An obscure passage from the sixteenth chapter of the book of Leviticus provides the origin of the term scapegoat. It's a person, group or thing forced to take the blame for the mistakes or crimes of others.

On the day of Atonement (tenth day of seventh month), the high priest took two goats and presented them to the lord. Lots were cast and the one upon which the Lord's lot fell was killed and offered up as a blood sacrifice for the sins of the people.

The remaining goat became the "scapegoat." After completing the sacrifice of the first one, the high priest laid both hands on the head of the live goat. He then confessed over it all of the iniquities and transgressions of the people, putting them on the head of the goat who was required to bear them.

A physically fit man then took the scapegoat deep into the wilderness--into an uninhabited land from which it could never return--and released it.

The children of Israel rejoiced as they watched this illustrated sermon of their sins being taken from them, never to be seen or heard from again.

Their sins were FORGIVEN by the sacrifice of the first goat, and FORGOTTEN by the transfer of them upon the second and its permanent banishment.

Through His death on the cross, Jesus both forgives and forgets our sins when we ask Him to do so. He then requires us to do likewise, and in fact built that into the prayer He taught His disciples. (Luke 11:4)

There may be a need to deal further with some offences simply for clarification, correction and prevention of future occurrences. But God will provide the opportunity and show us the proper manner for doing so if we sincerely forgive the offender.

Obeying Commandments Five Through Ten

The first four commandments found in Deuteronomy 5:6-15 deal with our relationship with God. Jesus referred to these as the First Great Commandment. (Matthew 22:37,38). The remaining six found in Deuteronomy 5:16-21 relate to how we are to treat others. The Lord refers to these as the Second Great Commandment.

When we honor and respect our parents, we in essence thank God for using them to give us life on earth and an opportunity to spend eternity in heaven with Him. And when we refuse to do physical harm to another, are faithful and true to our spouse, refuse to take that which doesn't belong to us, refrain from gossip and slander, and flee from the temptation of lusting for that which God has given to others, we reverence the Author of life. Refusing to do anything detrimental to those with whom we share this earth is as much an act of brotherly kindness as the many overt deeds performed on behalf of another.

Chapter Twenty Five   Just Being There

One of the greatest acts of kindness we can do for another is simply to be there during their times of grief. This generally requires no words nor actions, just our presence. This communicates our sincere concern for them as no expression could ever achieve.

As easy as it seems, this is one of the most difficult acts to perform. We make a hundred excuses such as "they need to be alone," or "I don't want to intrude on their privacy." The truth is, however, we don't want to be around sadness, despair, sorrow or pain. It reminds us that all of us must experience such times during this life. We therefore only wish to be near those that encourage and make us feel good.

Solomon tells us of the inevitable seasons of life when he says, "There is a time for everything, and a season for every activity under heaven. . .a time to weep and a time to laugh, a time to mourn and a time to dance" (Ecclesiastes 3:1&4). Paul instructs us to "Rejoice with those who rejoice; mourn with those who mourn" (Romans 12:15).

Those who have experienced heart-wrenching personal tragedies often reveal they don't know how they would have gotten thorough that terrible time without the precious friend who was always just there for them. Nothing anyone else gave, did for them or said came close to the love demonstrated by the compassionate one.

True acts of brotherly kindness require sensitivity and an unselfish spirit. We must ask God to give us discernment to know what the other person really wants or needs in any particular situation. Our diversity often causes that which would work best or be most appreciated by me in similar circumstances to fail to be beneficial to another. We must therefore get our eyes off ourselves and genuinely desire to be used of God to bless others.

Lesson Ten
Add Love to Brotherly Kindness

ON A SCENIC NEW HAMPSHIRE FARM, a chicken, cow and pig decided to have breakfast together the following morning. The chicken said, "I will provide the eggs;" and the cow said, "I will bring the milk." But when the pig made no such offer, the chicken and cow instructed him to provide the bacon.

The pig objected by saying, "you two are only willing to give gifts, but you want me to sacrifice my very self."

It would appear from the context of the 2 Peter 1:5-7 passage that the above story defines the difference between brotherly kindness and love. The former is the giving of time, energy, resources, affection and attention. The latter means to give without restraint or limitation; even of one's own life if necessary.

This is what Jesus did for us, and obviously is what He expects of his true disciples. The Lord said to the apostles, "My command is this: Love each other as I have loved you. Greater love has no one than this, that one lay down his life for his friends. You are my friends if you do what I command" (John 15: 12-14). This level of devotion, courage and commitment is thus the culmination of securing and developing faith, goodness, knowledge, self-control, perseverance, godliness and brotherly kindness.

Chapter Twenty Six Definition and Use

Webster defines love as "a deep and tender feeling of fondness and devotion." [1] A particular Bible dictionary, however, makes no such attempt to simplify this word's meaning. Referring to the various contexts in which we find love around 300 times in Scripture, it utilizes four pages and approximately 3,500 words [2].

Our culture uses and abuses the word love in a vociferous manner. Seldom does its expression or enactment conjure up images of selfless devotion, uncompromising commitment, sincerity or fidelity. It generally has to do with one's self gratification or fulfillment, and is most often the conditional form of love. This type simply says, "I will love you if you do this or are this for me." Even when it appears to be sustained, it often degenerates into an obsession, a possession or co-dependency.

The Christian community, in my opinion, often uses the word love in a compulsive and hypocritical manner. Many feel the need to repeatedly tell their fellow church members, Bible study friends, etc. that they love them. Yet true concern or appreciation for that person appears to be lacking much of the time.

God's Version of Love

Biblical love requires risk, work and courage. It demands vulnerability by extending ourselves into another's domain; that frightening experience of doing things differently and venturing into unfamiliar territory. Moving towards someone acquires the risk of that person moving away from us. The potential of hurt feelings, disappointment and heartache are ever-present when one dares to truly love another fallible human being.

Biblical love compels us to give priority to what's best for the other person over our own hopes and desires. Personal ambition, hidden agendas and self fulfillment cannot abide here. Yet a meaningful and significant life is not possible without relationships that give it purpose, and scratch the itch nothing else can reach. We can oppose our innate substance by seeking and serving substitutes, but we won't win this match since God created us this way.

An honest appraisal of my own life reflects a greater willingness to take physical risks than relational ones. I find that the courage to chance bodily injury is of a lesser degree than that required to risk heartache and rejection. But God never hesitates to make overtures to we who are so fragile, fickle and unfaithful; and He accordingly expects us to do no less

Paul put this commandment into a prayer for the believers at Ephesus. He said, "I pray that out of his glorious riches he may strengthen you with power through his Spirit in your inner being, so that Christ may dwell in your hearts through faith. And I pray that you, being rooted and established in love, may have power, together with all the saints, to grasp how wide and long and high and deep is the love of Christ, and to know this love that surpasses knowledge--that you may be filled to the measure of all the fullness of God" (Ephesians 3:16-19).

I'm grateful he makes it clear we cannot acquire or manufacture biblical love by our own abilities or resources. This saves me much frustration caused by the futility of attempting to ascend to a level not humanly possible. I can stop all my fruitless efforts at expressing and exhibiting something contrary to my nature. I must simply depend upon the Lord to fill me with His love that is then sufficient to flow onto others.

I am also happy to learn that God's brand of love is the power to achieve His purpose for me while on this earth. If true love was no more than the mushy, gushy emotional expression this world reduces it to, I would have no interest in it.

And I also appreciate knowing that the love that empowers me to perform tasks abundantly above and beyond my own capacities, surpasses knowledge. Thus I don't have to understand, define or explain it. And for that reason I will make no attempt to do so, but spend the remainder of this lesson on examples of biblical love.

Chapter Twenty Seven Rewards of Self Sacrifice

I read about Julius Hickerson, a promising young doctor who turned his back on aquiring wealth in the united States to answer God's call to the mission field. His friends felt his going to Columbia to treat the spirit and soul, as well as the body, was a foolish waste of his talent and education. He chose, however, to follow his heart rather than his ego.

There was little evidence of achieving his God-ordained purpose despite his tireless efforts for two years in Columbia. Then in 1951, as he attempted to take supplies to a remote village, he died in a plane crash.

As the natives searched the wreckage for anything of value, someone found a well highlighted Bible in their language. Several of them read it, got saved and started churches. They then went to other villages and preached the Gospel.

Some years later, having no knowledge of what took place there, the Southern Baptists sent a missionary to that region. He was surprised, to say the least, to find his mission field already evangelized. He inquired how this was possible without a missionary. The natives he asked showed him a Bible which had this notation on the inside cover: "Property of Julius Hickerson." [3]

Doing All He Could

I found in my file a revision of the following story. I don't recall the source, but it told of an American B-17 Flying Fortress on a bombing mission over Germany near the end of WWII. It took several hits from Nazi antiaircraft guns, with a few actually hitting the fuel tank. The crippled aircraft miraculously made it back to its home base without exploding or running out of fuel.

Eleven unexploded 20 millimeter shells were later carefully removed from the bomber. Each was dismantled and examined; and to everyone's amazement, all 11 were empty of explosive material. The mystery was solved when a note written in Czech was found inside one of the shells. Translated, it read, "This is all we can do for you now."   It is believed that a member of the Czech underground, working in a Nazi munitions factory, omitted the explosives in some of the shells on his or her assembly line. And in the hope that at least one of the allies who may benefit from those efforts would know they have friends behind enemy lines, he put an occasional note in one of the empty shells. And while they would never meet, an entire crew of a flying fortress was most grateful for his selfless love and willingness to risk grave consequences to save others.

Love of God and His Word

Pastor Charles Swindoll told the following story of the underground church in Russia prior to the Breakup of the Soviet Union.

A particular house church in a Russian city had just received a copy of Luke's Gospel, the only Scripture most of these Christians had ever seen. They tore it into small sections and distributed them among the body of believers. Their plan was to memorize the portion they had been given, then on the next Lord's Day they would meet and redistribute the scriptural sections.

On Sunday, these believers arrived inconspicuously in small groups throughout the day so as not to arouse the suspicion of KGB informers. By dusk they were all safely inside, windows closed and doors locked. They began by singing a hymn quietly but with deep emotion. Suddenly, the door was pushed open and in walked two soldiers with loaded automatic weapons at the ready. One shouted, "All right – everybody line up against the wall. If you wish to renounce your commitment to Jesus Christ, leave now!"

Two or three quickly left, then another. After a few more seconds, two more.

"This is your last chance. Either turn against your faith in Christ," he ordered, "or stay and suffer the consequences."

Another left. Finally, two more in embarrassed silence with their faces covered slipped out into the night. No one else moved. Parents with small children trembling beside them looked down reassuringly. They fully expected to be gunned down or, at best, to be imprisoned.

After a few moments of complete silence, the other soldier closed the door, looked back at those who stood against the wall and said, "Keep your hands up – but this time in praise to our Lord Jesus Christ, brothers and sisters. We, too, are Christians. We were sent to another house church several weeks ago to arrest a group of believers, but we were converted instead. We have learned by experience, however, that unless people are willing to die for their faith, they cannot be fully trusted." [4]

Those who remained, including the two soldiers, evidenced the power of the Holy Spirit in their inner being Paul spoke of in the above Ephesians passage. What else explains the courage and boldness for no earthly gain they exhibited?

Putting Others Ahead of Self

I read of a Japanese seashore village where an earthquake startled its inhabitants one autumn evening over a century ago. But being accustomed to earthquakes, they soon went back to their activities. Above the village on a high plain, an old farmer was watching from his house. He looked at the sea and saw that the water was dark and moving against the wind, running away from the land. The old man knew what it meant. His one thought was to warn the villagers.

He grabbed a torch and rushed to the fields behind his house. There lay his great crop of rice, piled in stacks ready for the market. Without hesitating he set fire to his fortune, and almost immediately the dry stalks were blazing. The big bell in the temple was soon tolling loudly.

Back from the beach, away from that strange sea, up the steep hill, came the people of the village. They were intent on saving the crops of their rich neighbor. As they reached the plain, the old man shouted back at the top of his voice, "Look!" At the edge of the horizon they saw a long, lean, dim line – a line that thickened as they gazed. That line was the sea, a tidal wave, rising like a high wall and coming more swiftly than a kite flies. Then came a shock, heavier than thunder. The great swell struck the shore with a weight that sent a shudder though the hills and tore their homes to shreds. It drew back, roaring. Then it struck again, and again, and yet again. Once more it struck and ebbed; then it returned to its place.

There was silence on the plain as they realized the old man standing among them was now about as poor as the rest of them. His wealth was gone, but his 400 neighbors remained because of the sacrifice he willingly and quickly make.*

Love Keeps Good Company

The story is told of a woman who saw three old men with long, white beards sitting on her front lawn. She went out and said to them, "I don't believe I know you gentlemen, but you must be hungry. Please come in and have something to eat." They responded by asking if the man of the house was at home. When the woman said no, they politely declined her invitation.

Her husband returned from work that evening and asked about the three old men in their front yard. His wife told him about their refusal to come in for something to eat without him being there. The husband then instructed her to extend the invitation once more.

When the woman went out to ask them in again, they replied that they don't enter a house together. "Why is that?," she asked. The spokesman for the group pointed to the old man on his left and said, "His name is Wealth." Then pointing to the other he said, "His name is Success, and I am Love." Then he added, "Please go in and discuss it with your husband as to which of us you wish to enter your home."

Upon being informed of the old man's instructions, the husband said, "This is great. Go out and invite Wealth into our home." But his wife disagreed, saying, "My dear, why don't we invite Success instead." Just then their daughter-in-law, who had overheard the conversation, walked into the room and suggested, "Wouldn't it be best to invite Love into our home and have it filled with love."

The husband, being somewhat embarrassed, said to his wife. "I think we should heed our daughter-in-law's advice. Please go out and invite Love to be our guest."

The woman went out and said to the three old men, "We have decided to invite Love into our home." Upon hearing that, Love got up and entered the house.

Wealth and Success likewise arose and followed him.

But the surprised woman said to the other two, "We only invited Love. Why are you two coming in also?" The three elders responded in unison, "When either Wealth or Success are invited, the other two of us stay out of that house. But when Love is invited, we all go in; because where there is love, there is also wealth and success."

Summary

The heroes in the above stories demonstrate love by denying self and defying human logic to do what pleases God and blesses or serves others. I am not confident, given those circumstances, I would have acted likewise. But I'm working on it. 2 Peter 1:5-7 encourages us to pursue the qualities expounded upon in this book in an ever increasing measure until we are consumed by biblical love. It's obvious that achieving and maintaining spirit, soul, and body fitness is essential for their attainment.

There are two types of love; the love of feeling and love which is willed. The former involves the emotions and changes like the weather, while the latter involves a decision to love no matter the circumstances; and is that which is essential for obeying the first and second great commandments. Referring to lesson one's trichotomy lesson, we see that true biblical love is a product of the soul existing only when the will is strongly influenced by a healthy spirit.

Most of the traits covered in the previous chapters are direct conditioned responses produced by efforts made for their achievement. Love, however, is for the most part indirect as it evolves or occurs from our drawing ever closer to the Lord through daily communion with Him. It is therefore both a conditioned response and natural reflex, evidenced primarily by our manner of thinking, speaking and doing.

Love is the essential ingredient for a healthy soul because it motivates us to study God's way of doing and being which energizes the mind, emotions and will. And love requires a healthy body, at least within the confines of any existing disability or uninvited affliction, because it demands a persistent course of action in serving others.

Scripture teaches love is the requisite condition from which the remaining fruit of the Spirit flows. It says, "But the fruit of the Spirit is love, joy, peace, patience, kindness, goodness, faithfulness, gentleness, and self-control" (Galatians 5:22). Life's experiences demonstrate that the above traits are exhibited only by those with the love of God and others in their heart.

The Bible likewise instructs that all of the wonderful gifts emanating from Holy Spirit filled believers are worthless without love. Paul tells us that those who speak in tongues, prophesy future events, understand mysteries hidden to finite minds, possess deep and penetrating knowledge, and have mountain-moving faith are nothing if they have not love. He states further that those who give all they have to the less fortunate and even their very life for a just cause, but are motivated by something other than love, gain nothing. (I Corinthians 13:1-3)

Just as the remaining Fruit of the Spirit are love's ever-present companions, envy, boasting, pride, rudeness, self-seeking, anger, unforgiveness and evil will never be found where love abides. As a result, those who love God and their fellow man rejoice in the truth, protect those whom God places in their care, trusts others, always hopes and perseveres, and never fails. (1Corinthians 13:4-8)

And in conclusion, faith, hope and love remain when all else ceases to exist. "But the greatest of these is love." (I Corinthians 13:13)

CONCLUSION

No one in America needs to read or hear another word regarding our current and potentially calamitous state of affairs. But we all need to see the big picture and the most disturbing trend it reveals.

In his Come Before Winter, Pastor Charles Swindoll says, "The history of great civilizations reminds me of a giant revolving door. It turns on the axis of human depravity as its movement is marked by the perimeter of time. With monotonous repetition each civilization has completed the same cycle, having passed through a similar sequence of events. It could be visualized like this:

From bondage to spiritual faith

From spiritual faith to great courage

From great courage to strength

From strength to liberty

From liberty to abundance

From abundance to leisure

From leisure to selfishness

From selfishness to complacency

From complacency to apathy

From apathy to dependency

From dependency to weakness

From weakness back to bondage"

Where would you say we are at this point? Keep in mind that when you're on a downward swing, gravity increases the speed of the descent.

In the same section, Pastor Swindoll quotes eighteenth century Professor Alexander Tyler speaking of the fall of the Athenian Republic. He said. "A democracy cannot exist as a permanent form of government. It can only exist until the voters discover they can vote themselves excessive gratuities from the public treasury. From that moment on the majority always votes for the candidates promising the most benefits from the treasury, with the result that a democracy collapses over loose fiscal policy, always followed by a dictatorship." [1]

Something Smells Around Here

I read of a bizarre experiment conducted on ants. Harvard biologist Edward O. Wilson noticed that it took ants a few days to recognize that a crumpled nestmate was dead. It became obvious that determination was made by smell, not sight. As the ant's decomposing body emitted a particular odor, other ants dutifully carried it out to a refuse pile.

Dr. Wilson eventually identified the chemical released by the dead ant as oleic acid. He daubed a bit of paper with it, and sure enough it got carried out to the ant cemetary. He then painted a live ant with oleic acid. Despite its legs and antennae wriggling vigorously in protest, it was seized and discarded in the same manner. And only when the indignant ant was able to rid itself of every trace of oleic acid, was it permitted to return to the nest. [2]

Far too many of our citizens have died spiritually because they have neglected or drifted away from their religious training or heritage. Far too many have died mentally because they replaced reading and thinking with hours on end in front of the television. Far too many have died emotionally because they lost the passion of experiencing life involved with others. And far too many are near dead physically due to excessive and/or unhealthy food intake, stress, and lack of exercise. They have the smell of death about them, are doing nothing to impact their world, and thus are being carried away by false belief systems, politicians with hidden agendas, and others who promise them something for nothing. If this defines any aspect of your life, it's time to remove all trace of that smell.

It's Not Too Late

The ostrich is an incredible creature. While classified as a bird, it can't fly. The males grow to a height of up to eight feet, can weigh as much as three hundred pounds, and run at a speed approaching forty miles per hour. But they are not too bright. This big bird doesn't bury its head in the sand as fabled, but puts its long neck and head on the ground to hide from suspected danger; oblivious to the full exposure of its huge body. And the females of the specie often leave their three pound eggs in the sand unprotected.

It's time to be mindful of current circumstances, existing trends, and how history is repeating itself. Peace and prosperity have never been permanent because they change people. The character traits and course of action that produced them are the first to go once leisure, the start of the downward turn, becomes the primary concern.

It's time to get in shape, get our heads off the sand, and protect ourselves and those depending on us. We need to be physically fit as we may lose some creature comforts and devices that do our work for us; be required to do jobs we pay others to do now; and take jobs of a manual labor nature. We need to be mentally and emotionally healthy as there will be tough decisions to make and people looking to us for direction.

Most importantly, we need to be in top shape spiritually. When things around us are changing or collapsing, the God Who is the same yesterday, today and tomorrow will be our anchor. His Word provides absolute truth and reliable guidance in good times or bad. His Holy Spirit will abide within us and give us godly wisdom and courage if we ask Him for it. His angels will surround and protect us, and those we love. And His light will lead us through the dark days and perilous nights.

You can count on the Lord doing His part if you do yours. SO GET MOVING!

About the Author

Thomas B. Geier, a Pennsylvania Certified Public Accountant, has been a devoted Bible student for decades. He practices and teaches the importance of comprehending and applying Scriptural principles and precepts to all areas of life – spiritual, mental, emotional, volitional, physical, relational and occupational – experiencing God's abundant blessings in each. Tom, his wife Connie, their three adult children and seven grandchildren are all serving the Lord.

Endnotes

LESSON 1

1   Phillip Keller; A Shepherd Looks At The Good Shepherd And His Sheep, Copyright
    (c) 1978, Inspirational Press, A division of Budget Book Service, Inc., 386 Park
    Avenue South, New York, NY 10016, Pp. 46-47. Geier Survival Training For The
    Believer 165

2   Oswald Chambers; My Utmost For His Highest; September 10th Devotion;
    Copyright (c) 1935 by Dodd Mead & Co., renewed 1963 by the Oswald Chambers
    Publication Association Ltd.

3   The Open Bible Expanded Edition; Thomas Nelson Publishers, 1983; P. 1,294.

4   Lauran Neergard; "Mental Exercise Crucial To Slowing Brain Decay;" The
    Associated Press; 7/30/2000 edition of the Pittsburgh Post Gazette.

5   Dennis Prager; An interview by The Door entitled "A Civilization That Believes In
    Nothing;" November/December, 1990 edition; P. 15.

6   From Disciplines Of A Godly Man by R. Kent Hughes; Copyright (c) 1991, P. 73.
    Used by permission of Crossway Books, a division of Good News Publishers,
    Wheaton, Illinois, 60187.

7   James C. McKinley, Jr.; "Sports Fan The Flames;" The New York Times;
    8/11/2000 edition of the Pittsburgh Post Gazette.

8   Thomas Kelley; A Testament Of Devotion; P. 115.

9   Richard J. Foster; Freedom Of Simplicity; Harper Paperbacks 1998; P. 101-102.

10 Peter Marshall & David Manuel;The Light And The Glory; Fleming H. Revell, a
    division of Baker Book House Company (c) 1977, P. 325.

LESSON 2

1   Dr. Alfred L. Heller; Your Body, His Temple; Thomas Nelson Publishers, 1981.

2   Taken from Honest To God/ by Bill Hybels. Copyright (c) 1990 by Bill Hybles. Used by Permission of Zondervan Publishing House. Pp. 167-168.

3   Lauran Neergard; "Mental Exercise Crucial To Slowing Brain Decay;" The Associated Press; 7/30/2000 edition of the Pittsburgh Post Gazette.

4   The American Medical Association Home Medical Encyclopedia; Published in 1989 by The Reader's Digest Association, Inc., with permission of Random House, Inc.; P. 738. Geier Survival Training For The Believer 166

5   Dr. Alfred L. Heller; (See 1 Above); Pp. 142-143 & 147.

6   President's Council on Physical Fitness and Sports, 400 6th Street, S.W., Washington, D.C. 20201.

7   Dr. Alfred L. Heller; (See 1 Above); Pp. 37-38.

8   Bill Hybels; (See 2 Above); P. 174.

LESSON 3

1   Webster's New World Dictionary, Elementary Edition; 1961; P. 255.

2   The New Compact Bible Dictionary; 1967; P. 169.

3   Prelude to the Book of Joshua; The Open Bible Expanded Edition; Thomas Nelson Publishers, 1983; P. 209.

4   Breakpoint with Chuck Colson; Copyright (c) 2000 Prison Fellowship Ministries; Commentary # 000825.

5   Breakpoint with Chuck Colson; Copyright (c) 2000 Prison Fellowship Ministries; Commentary # 000904.

6   Breakpoint with Chuck Colson; Copyright (c) 2000 Prison Fellowship Ministries; Commentary # 000829.

7   Gregg Easterbrook; July 25, 1999 edition of the Pittsburgh Post Gazette.

LESSON 4

1   From George Whitefield by Arnold A. Dallimore; Copyright (c) 1990; P. 181. Used by permission of Crossway Books, a division of Good News Publishers, Wheaton, Illinois 60187.

2   Taken from Motivation To last A Lifetime by Theodore W. Engstrom. Copyright (c) 1984 by the Zondervan Corporation. Used by permission of Zondervan Publishing House. Pp. 58-60.

3   The Open Bible Expanded Edition; Thomas Nelson Publishers, 1983; P. 622 Geier Survival Training For The Believer 167

4   From; Maranatha: Our Lord Come!--A Definitive Study of the Rapture of the Church by Renald Showers (c) 1995; Pp. 243 & 255-56. Used by permission of The Friends of Israel Gospel Ministry, Inc., Bellmar, NJ.

LESSON 5

1   Heard on Pittsburgh, PA radio station WJAS in fall of 1997. The source of the study was not provided.

2   From Take A Break by Robert J. Strand (c) 1992, Pp. 130-31. Used by permission of The Gospel Publishing House, 1445 Boonville Avenue, Springfield, MO 65802-1894.

3   From Autobiography Of God by Lloyd John Ogilvie (c) 1979; P. 56. Used by permission of Gospel Light / Regal Books, Ventura, CA 93003.

4   Ray Comfort; Russia Will Attack Israel; The Thinking Mind Publications, 1991; Pp. 117-120.

5   Taken from A Layman Looks At The Lord's Prayer by Phillip Keller. Used by permission of Moody Press (c) 1976, Pp. 188-198.

6   Taken from Come Before Winter And Share My Hope by Charles R. Swindoll, Copyright (c) 1985 by Charles R. Swindoll, Inc. Used by permission of Zondervan Publishing House. Pp. 297-98.

7   John C. Hagee; Beginning Of The End; Thomas Nelson, Inc., 1996; Pp 86-87.

LESSON 6

1   2 & 3) Taken from What's So Amazing About Grace by Philip D. Yancey, Copyright (c) 1997 by Philip d. Yancey, Used by permission of Zondervan Publishing House, P. 31-32. Geier Survival Training For The Believer 168

2   4) Herbert B. Brooks; Prime Time; Thomas Nelson, Inc. Publishers, 1978; Pp. 102-104.

3   5) Charles H. Spurgeon; Words Of Wisdom; 1993; Pp. 72-75. Used by permission of the publisher, Whitaker House, 30 Hunt Valley Circle, New kensington, PA 15068.

4   6) From Take A Break by Robert J. Strand (c) 1992, Pp. 138-39. Used by permission of The Gospel Publishing House, 1445 Boonville Avenue, Springfield, MO 65802- 1894.

5   Oswald Chambers; My Utmost For His Highest; December 5th Devotion; Copyright (c) 1935 by Dodd Mead & Co., renewed 1963 by Oswald Chambers Publication Association Ltd.

LESSON 7

1   Robert Strand; Just For Fathers; Access Publishing, 1994; Pp. 60-61.

2   Living Above The Level Of Mediocrity; Charles R. Swindoll; 1990; Pp. 147-49; Word Publishing, Nashville, Tennessee. All rights reserved.

3   From Autobiography of God by Lloyd John Ogilvie (c) 1979, Pp. 117-18. Used by permission of Gospel Light/Regal Books, Ventura, CA 93003.

4   Anna Robertson Brown; What Is Worthwhile; Written during the 19th century; Publisher and page numbers unknown.

5   M. Scott Peck; Further Along the Road Less Travelled; New York: Simon & Schuster, 1993; P. 167.

LESSON 8

1   Taken from Come Before Winter And Share My Hope by Charles R. Swindoll. Copyright (c) 1985 by Charles R. Swindoll, Inc. Used by permission of Zondervan Publishing House. P. 83. Geier Survival Training For The Believer 169

2   Bill Hull; Jesus Christ Disciple-Maker; Navpress, 1984; Pp. 116-17.

3   Pat Robertson; The Secret Kingdom; Bantam Books/Thomas Nelson, Inc., 1982.

4   Living On The Ragged Edge; Charles R. Swindoll, 1985; Word Publishing, Nashville, Tennessee. All rights Reserved.

5   Taken from Honest To God? by Bill Hybels. Used by permission of Zondervan Publishing House. Pp. 12 and 177-90.

6   Benjamin B. Warfield; Counterfeit Miracles; The Banner Of Truth Trust, 1918, reprint 1972; Pp. 235-36 and 6.

7   Jack S. Deer; Surprised By The Power Of The Spirit; Zondervan Publishing House, 1993.

LESSON 9

1   Taken from Honest To God? by Bill Hybles. Copyright (c) 1990 by Bill Hybles. Used by permission of Zondervan Publishing House. Pp.75-77.

2   Alan Loy McGinnis; Bringing Out The Best In People; Augsburg Publishing House, 1985; Pp. 75-77.

3   Charles R. Swindoll; "Wheaton Alumni" August/September, 1991 publiction; P. 5.

4   Steve Farrar; Finishing Strong: Multnomah Books, 1995; Pp. 33-35.

LESSON 10

1   Webster's New World Dictionary, Elementary Edition; 1961; P. 416.

2   John L. McKensie: Dictionary Of The Bible; The Bruce Publishing Company, 1965; Pp.520-523.

3   Robert Strand; Just For Fathers; Access Publishing, 1994; Pp. 30-31

4   Living Above The Level Of Mediocrity; Charles R. Swindoll, 1990; Pp. 57-58; Word Publishing, Nashville, Tennessee. All rights reserved. Geier Survival Training For The Believer 170

CONCLUSION

1   Taken from Come Before Winter And Share My Hope by Charles R. Swindoll. Copyright (c) 1985 by Charles R. Swindoll, Inc. Used by permission of Zondervan Publishing House. Pp. 321-22.

2   Philip Yancey; What's So Amazing About Grace?; Zondervan Publishing House, 1997; Pp 186-87.

www.ingramcontent.com/pod-product-compliance
Lightning Source LLC
LaVergne TN
LVHW061222060426
835509LV00012B/1387